With love &
blessings!
Angie
8/11

FOCUS
Families Of Children United In Spirit
A group no one wants to belong to . . .

Spiritual journeys of families after the loss of a loved one

Regina Elkhatib

Angela Christensen

authorHOUSE®

AuthorHouse™
1663 Liberty Drive
Bloomington, IN 47403
www.authorhouse.com
Phone: 1-800-839-8640

First published by AuthorHouse   07/25/2011

ISBN: 978-1-4634-3680-3 (sc)
ISBN: 978-1-4634-3681-0 (ebk)

Printed in the United States of America

Any people depicted in stock imagery provided by Thinkstock are models, and such images are being used for illustrative purposes only.
Certain stock imagery © Thinkstock.

This book is printed on acid-free paper.

Because of the dynamic nature of the Internet, any web addresses or links contained in this book may have changed since publication and may no longer be valid. The views expressed in this work are solely those of the author and do not necessarily reflect the views of the publisher, and the publisher hereby disclaims any responsibility for them.

CONTENTS

As a bereaved mother of Chelsey Erin Valle, who at age seven, died as a result of a car accident, I know that only another bereaved parent can truly understand what I was going through. I have come to believe that part of the gift Chelsey gave me, in her passing, was the opportunity to educate others about bereaved parents, for only in understanding us, can they support and help us through our grief. We are never taught how to grieve. Society would rather ignore bereaved parents because they are scared to try to understand us.

I think that this book is a wonderful portrayal of how diverse, yet similar their stories are. In reading them, they help shine a light on all bereaved parent's struggle to come out of the dark lonely tunnel of grief. We must learn how to become a new person. I call it my "after Chelsey." Regina and Angela should be proud of bringing these stories together in a wonderfully moving book that shows the readers an inside glimpse of dealing with the grief of losing a loved one.

Sue Valle
Facilitator
Bereaved Parents Support Group
Perrysburg, Ohio

The authors tell their stories with such compassion and honesty that it captures the heart. Through my years at Hospice, I have witnessed the power of God meeting people in their journey of sorrows, bringing them comfort and peace.

Kathy Goetz, MA LPC
Retired Director of Bereavement Services
Hospice of Lenawee
Adrian, Michigan

We dedicate this book to you, Mark and Nick.

With your passings, our beliefs were challenged, our reality expanded, our spirituality grew and we realized our love was eternal.

From Angela:

I also dedicate this book to my best friend, my high school sweetheart, my soul mate, and my husband, Mark, who passed away suddenly and quietly during the writing of this book. He was my strength, my confidante, and my support for over thirty years.
He and Nick are now together.

Mark Andrew Christensen

9/13/57 – 1/10/09

ACKNOWLEDGMENTS

A FRIEND

I need a friend to sit with
To help me struggle through
The sadness and the anger,
The crying I must do.

I need a friend to sit with
To help me work this out,
The guilt and all the anguish
To times I want to shout.

I need a friend to sit with
To help me through my pain,
The longing and the emptiness
The need to speak his name.

—Lilly Barstow

First and foremost, we are grateful to those who contributed to this book. We cannot find words to adequately thank the mothers, fathers, grandparents, siblings and friends who were willing to bare their souls and mentally return to the darkest days of their lives in the hope of helping other grieving families. We know this was no small task, and this was done by them to honor their loved ones and to keep their memories alive.

To Lena Elkhatib, thank you for designing our cover. Your artistic talent conveyed the first impression we wanted for our book. We know this was your way of honoring your cousin, Mark.

We wish to thank Perry and Linda Johnson, Brenda Cody, and Danielle Wurzell for editing our stories. We can't thank you enough for your love and support.

To Ginny Sussman, whose photographic skills enabled us to give our readers an image of our loved ones as we had envisioned.

We are very grateful to Barbara Steck for her compassion and help through HUGS (Helping Unexpected Grief Survivors).

Rob Salem, we thank you for your legal expertise and your love for your nephew, Mark.

We want to express our gratitude to John Turski for his spiritual guidance and connection to our sons, Mark and Nick.

The support of family is very important. We would like to thank our husbands, Mounir and Mark for their love and encouragement. Our children, Dina, Rick, Danya, Eric and Amanda—you gave us a reason to go on with life. Thank you for choosing us as your mothers.

Mark and Nick, you have inspired us from your spiritual world. Your short lives, free spirits, and wisdom beyond your years have propelled us into our new lives. You taught us to continue to live our lives to the fullest. This book is to honor you. We love you so very much.

INTRODUCTION

By Regina Elkhatib and Angela Christensen

We met in the fall of 2001 at a FOCUS bereavement support group meeting. Coming from two different backgrounds, it seemed as if the only thing we had in common was we each had lost a son in an auto accident. Within moments of our first conversation, we both knew we were kindred souls. We knew our sons had brought us together.

It didn't take us long to realize we had similar spiritual beliefs. Even though we came from different religious backgrounds, each of our independent life experiences had brought us to the same spiritual conclusions. Losing our sons had thrust us into a deeper spiritual awakening.

Regina: On May 26, 1976 my son, Mark, came into my life making it complete. On June 18, 1996 he was taken in an instant, leaving me shattered and grief stricken. My mere existence was questionable at times. Slowly, over the months, I realized I had to make a decision. Mark cannot be forgotten. I needed to do something to honor him.

After attending a bereavement group in Perrysburg, Ohio, my husband, Mounir and I decided to form our own group. FOCUS was started in March, 1998. We have been meeting ever since helping ourselves and others. By helping others

1

through their grief, we formed close friendships that will last a lifetime. With help and guidance from the universe, my world finally became brighter and more meaningful. I knew I had to go on. Thank you, Mark, for helping me to go forward and not quit. It is an honor to be your mother. I love you.

Angela: As far back as I can remember, the only thing I knew for certain in my life was that I wanted to be a mother. So when my son, Nick, was born March 24, 1982, it was one of the happiest days of my life. It is truly a blessing I did not know at that time what life had in store for me. One single moment on July 19, 2001, changed everything. Nick was gone. What an imprint he left on this planet. What an imprint he left on my heart and soul.

When I met Regina, her first words to me were, "When I read your son, Nick's obituary in the newspaper, I knew I would be meeting you." And so began our journey together. Through the many waves of grief, agonizing pain and despair, Regina and other members of FOCUS were there to continuously help and support me. I survived Nick's death in large part because of this bond and the friendships I would make. Sharing my grief with others who had the same loss helped me survive and brought me hope.

I never could have imagined the life I'm living now, having survived the death of my child. I feel Nick's life and even his death were gifts from him for my spiritual growth. I am thankful and honored to have shared this lifetime together with him. I will always love you, Nick.

To those of you who have lost a loved one, our goal is that this collection of personal stories will bring you hope. You are not alone. Many have walked your path and know the true depth of your sorrow. Our wish is that these stories will resonate with you and healing will begin. With that healing, we wish you hope for the future. With hope, your future will someday include being reunited with your loved one.

Our message is simple. Your loved one is closer to you in spirit than you can ever imagine. Through the darkness of grief, know there will come a day when you will feel the warmth of sunshine, hear the joy of laughter and taste life with a new perspective.

To those of you who have not lost a loved one, our desire is that you gain understanding of the bereaved. We hope our stories speak to your soul. We offer you insight that may help you gain compassion and sympathy for those who are grieving.

ONE STEP

By Marilyn Heavilin

Take one step, just one step
That's all you need to do today.
Take one step, just one little step
By reaching out your hand to someone else.
Some of us have walked this path before you.
It's a rough path, a tough path,
But we can make it.
Hang on to me and I'll hang on to you.
We may stumble, we may even fall,
But we'll start with just one step,
Your hands linked with mine.
Yes, we can make it.
All of us together,
Just one step at a time.

MY MARKIE

It Is An Honor To Be Your Mother

By Regina Elkhatib

The Happiest Days of My Life

The last thirteen years of my life have been like a movie. Rewind to May 26, 1976 when my husband, Mounir and I celebrated the birth of our third child, Mark Khaled Elkhatib. His middle name means 'eternal' in Arabic. That day was one of the happiest of my life. Dina was our oldest child at four years and Ricky was two. Needless to say my hands were full when Markie came along, yet we went on to have another daughter, Danya, two years later. Two girls and two boys, how perfect! I was a full-time mom. Mounir's medical practice was growing and everyone was healthy. That was all that mattered. We were very content.

Each of our children had distinct personalities. Dina was quiet and stubborn. With her, everything had to be in its rightful place. Ricky was a serious and intelligent bookworm. Danya, the baby of the family, was sensitive and loving and displayed her qualities intensely. Then there was Markie.

Though definitely our wild child, he was also caring. He would not let anyone be angry with him for any length of time, and his own anger was usually short lived. Like the rest of the kids, Mark had a normal childhood, though he was quite accident prone. If Markie had a hangnail, out came the arm sling. A scraped knee meant a dig through the basement for crutches. Mark would do anything for attention and he usually got it.

Markie made average grades in school only because he would do exactly what was expected of him and no more. He was the clown of the class. I remember on teacher conference days, Mounir and I would argue over who would go to Ricky's classroom and who would take Mark's. It was always a toss up; would his teacher comment on his constant talking? Or would it be his fidgeting? Maybe it would be his not following directions that would be the issue this time?

Mounir and I had a strange inner-knowing about Mark, especially as he got older. We let him do things that his siblings were never allowed to do. He was the only child who went on spring break to Florida, for instance. And when he was eighteen, we let him go to California with his best friend, Doug. When he wanted to form a band, we shopped for a drum set the next day. One Saturday morning, Mark called me. "Mom, I found the neatest car! Can you and dad come to look at it?!" It was a black Trans Am, a little sports car that made me very nervous. He read my face. "Look!" Mark said, "The driver's side door is even reinforced with a steel rod." We co-signed. "I love you Mom and Dad. You've made me the happiest person alive!" Mark told us. Then he kissed us both.

During his second year in the College of Business at the University of Toledo, Mark held down a job at a restaurant. He was also on the board of the Huntington Community Center in Sylvania, Ohio which helps people in need in our area. Mark served as a teen representative. He was a happy, well-liked young man with a very busy social life, yet he always made time to spend with his family. Life was good.

Around this time, a family relative's twenty-one year old son, Sam, came from Canada to stay with us for an extended length of time. Instantly, Sam was drawn to Mark and clung to him around the clock. Mark became uncomfortable with this soon after Sam arrived, and we had a wonderful, long talk about it one evening. Afterward, I kissed him goodnight and told him that I loved him. He naturally did the same. It was the last conversation I had with my son. For that, I will be eternally grateful.

The Day My Heart Broke

The eighteenth of June, 1996, was a hot and rainy Tuesday. Mounir had left for Lebanon two days prior to visit family. That day, I made dinner plans with some of my friends. One of them, Mona, was in town from Missouri. We always had fun when she visited, so I was looking forward to our get-together that much more. Just after 3:00 p.m., Mona and I were sitting at the kitchen table. The phone rang. It was Sam's mother from Canada. She hurriedly said, "I just received a call from Toledo Hospital telling me that Sam was in an accident!" My heart stopped. Mark was in his car with Sam that day. I asked if she knew anything about Mark. She did not. I hung up the phone and told Mona that my son was gone.

Since I could not bear to, Mona made several calls to the hospital before she could get any kind of information about Mark. Eventually, she was told that I should just go there. In my heart, I knew what had happened. I called my parents to pick me up. The car ride was endless. When we did arrive at the hospital, a nurse ushered us into a small, frigid room where a social worker was waiting to give us the unbearable news. My Markie was gone in an instant. Sam, however, simply opened his door and walked away without a scratch. I remember feeling very, very cold. Another good friend, Maryse, happened to be visiting someone at the hospital. Somehow she heard about Mark and made her way into our private waiting room. I recall placing my head in her lap while she covered me with warm blankets that did not calm my shivering.

Once back home, I found our house full. Thankfully, my parents, brothers and so many close friends stepped forward to take over. Dina, Ricky and Danya surrounded me, as well, and I was especially thankful for them. Mounir was on his thirteen-hour flight to return home. I could hardly wait to see him, and was terribly worried about his safety on the plane.

I don't remember who finally told me the details of Mark's accident. He lost control of his beloved Trans Am on wet pavement and hit a tree just two blocks from my parent's home. The driver's side took the impact. The "reinforced" door had not protected him. Mark would always make us give him a dime if we did not fasten our seat belts, but this day he was not wearing his. The paramedics reassured us, however, that it would not have changed the outcome. I have always wondered what his last thoughts were and if he knew what was happening. I've heard that the soul leaves the body before the actual impact, so I have to believe he did not suffer.

Mounir came home the following day to a mob of loved ones all trying to help us in any way. What could they do? Nothing helped at the time. All I wanted was to hug my baby boy and see his beautiful face. I do not remember much of what went on at the time. There is one thing I do recall clearly and that was asking for my friend, Najat, who was vacationing in Florida. She was the only person I knew who had lost a child. Her son, Jimmy, passed three years earlier as a result of a heart attack. Without hesitation, she came home to be with us.

Mark's funeral was huge. People we did not even know came to pay their respects to a young man who had touched so many lives. Until then, we had no idea of all the thoughtful things he had done for others along the way. In hindsight, I wish I'd recorded all of the beautiful stories that were shared with us. They were so comforting and typical of Markie. He would give wholeheartedly again and again, never intending to receive.

A few weeks after the funeral, visits from friends dwindled and I understood that. They had to get on with their lives, even though mine was halted in time. Mounir had to return to work, the children went to school, and I felt horribly alone. My parents never left me, though. They were grieving, too. I truly did not think I could survive, nor did I want to. Everything reminded me of my son . . . the grocery store, the mall, restaurants, everywhere I went. I watched people laughing and enjoying themselves and I wanted to yell, "Don't you know what happened?! How can you be happy?" Fortunately, my bouts of rage did not last long. I found out that many people did love and care about me. Coming to that realization caused me to pick myself up and, once again, take care of my family. That, I knew, Markie would want.

Signs of Hope

I am often asked how many children I have. In the beginning stages of my grief, it was very difficult to respond. Mark wasn't here anymore, but for twenty years, he was. He is not here in the physical, but in spirit. How could I erase him? Mark is and always will be my son. When I am asked that question, I am flooded with every emotion a person can go through in one lifetime; joy that I had Mark, heartbreak, sadness and on and on. Yet I've survived, and now I respond without hesitation, "I have four children, two girls and two boys, though I lost one of my sons in a car accident."

One of the things that helped me cope most was reading. Someone gave me a book written by George Anderson entitled, "We Don't Die". I wasn't at all sure that I could concentrate enough to read, but after only a few pages, I soaked up every word like a sponge. George Anderson is a medium. After starting the book, I discovered that a medium is a person who channels the spirits of those who have crossed over. These were true readings with real people who had lost loved ones. Though I had never heard of readings or mediums before, I held fast to the concept. At that time, I grasped onto anything and everything that might help keep me afloat. After I finished that book, I read three more written by Anderson. I knew not to tell anyone. "Poor Regina," they might say or, "She is really losing it." I kept my reading to myself, mostly doing so at night time. As I poured over my books, I began to have dreams or "visitations" from Mark. Unlike most people in my situation, night time was my salvation. My books, my dreams . . . I knew my Markie was nearby.

My friend, Joyce, invited a young girl to her house. Lisa was a medium. I was anxious to meet with her *and* skeptical. On my way to Joyce's, I asked Mark to mention my aching wisdom tooth just to prove her legitimacy. I sat down with Lisa in a small room. She held my hand and prayed. A couple of moments later, she looked up at the corner of the room and said, "O.K., I'll tell her." Then directing her attention toward me she said, "He's saying, 'Mom, get that tooth fixed'." After my first encounter with a medium I was convinced that "we don't die." After that, I went to several other mediums as well. They all told me that Mark was working on the other side. His job was to help cross children over. I can understand why he would choose that. He loved children so much and they loved him.

Mark adored his little niece, Kayla, who was ten months old at the time of his passing. We never let her forget her uncle,

12

and we told her that he was her guardian angel. When Kayla was about two and a half, we heard her talking to someone. With no one else in her room, I asked who it was that she was talking to. Her reply was simple. "Uncle Mark is telling me how much he loves me." That was the beginning of her conversations with him. Once, Mounir had Kayla on his lap. It was a difficult evening for him as he was really missing Mark. She asked her grandfather what was wrong with him. "I'm just having a sad time, Kayla," he told her. We had a large photograph of Mark over our fireplace. Kayla put her little hand on Mounir's face and turned it toward the picture. "He's saying he loves you," she said.

Kayla continued communicating with her Uncle Mark until she was six or seven years old. I've read that children and animals are not clouded with life's problems, so spirits find it simpler to communicate through them. To be honest, Kayla's ability made me jealous. I wanted to be the one who saw and spoke to Mark. One day, however, I got my wish. I was playing peek-a-boo with Kayla in our driveway next to our car. For an instant, I saw Mark's face in the left corner of the car's window. I froze. Mounir immediately noticed and asked what was wrong. "I think I saw an apparition of Mark in that window," I told him. He said matter-of-factly, "You know, it is Mother's Day." I am a firm believer that our loved ones are always around us.

Now I am convinced that Mark is with me every step of the way. When I am down and feel like I can't continue, it is he who picks me up and pushes me forward. Two weeks before his accident, Mark gave me his favorite Billy Joel CD. Now, every time I hear one of the songs, I sense Mark listening along with me. Even the ring tone on my cell phone is "Only the Good Die Young". That was Mark's favorite.

Another sign that convinces me of his presence happened about three months after Mark passed. In our basement, Mark had his own little "apartment" that had a kitchen, bathroom and a bedroom. One day, I went down there to feel close to him. As I was going through his things, I found a poetry book. One of the pages was folded over, so I turned to that poem. The title of it jumped out at me! It was called, "To My Parents." It was about a child telling his parents how much he appreciates and loves them even though he didn't say it enough.

Honoring Mark

In the Islamic faith, the best way to honor your loved ones is to set up an ongoing charity in his or her name. This was very important to me. My fear was that people would forget Mark . . . his face, his voice and the impact that he had on his family and friends. Mounir and I set up a scholarship fund immediately at the Islamic Center of Greater Toledo. We also began attending a bereavement group to help us through our darkest days.

The group was held on the second Tuesday of each month. I would have gone everyday had it been offered. The bereavement group is where I met Brenda. She lost her son, Rick, to Leukemia a year after Mark's passing. Over the months, we became good friends and we both had the idea of somehow honoring our sons in a way that would help children in our community. Brenda and I created "Four the Boys Foundation" in 2004.

A slow start to building our foundation did nothing to dampen our spirits. We held fundraisers, dances and silent auctions. We also held "spiritual days." These were open houses for the public where we gathered intuitive readers, mediums, massage therapists and other spiritual talents. Soon, the causes began presenting themselves to us. To our pleasure, Brenda and I were able to help charities both large and small. Among them were the Sunshine Children's Home, leukemia research, the Y.W.C.A Battered Women's Shelter, and the Assistance Dogs of America program. It was hard work and we were proud of what we had accomplished.

Another project that Mounir and I were invested in was beginning of our own bereavement group. F.O.C.U.S. (Families of Children United in Spirit) was formed. Our friend, Joyce (who had lost her daughter, Jennifer) wanted to help us. F.O.C.U.S. was put into action in short order, and we began meeting at Flower Hospital on the fourth Thursday of every month. We wanted people to be able to attend both the Tuesday group and our meetings, if they felt the need. Unfortunately, new members added themselves to the meetings each month. We always start out our meetings by saying, *"This is the club that no one wants to belong to."* Most formed close friendships. Many went on to honor their loved ones in varying ways that will become evident as you continue reading our stories.

One morning, about five years into F.O.C.U.S., I was reading the obituaries. A 19 year-old boy had perished in a car accident. His name was Nick Christensen. I read about him and thought how much he reminded me of Mark. I knew I would meet his mother and shortly afterward my premonition came true. Angela arrived at our group. I sat next to her knowing full well that we would connect strongly, just as I had known with Brenda. A few years later, during a meeting after a member finished sharing her story, I mentioned that although the details varied, our commonalities were the same. At that moment Angie (as I came to know her) and I looked at each other. Our thoughts were identical. We were to write a book. Our book was intended to help parents and siblings during their unbearable journeys.

It has been quite a few years since I lost my Markie. Though it is difficult at times, I've learned to live a new life without him. I am still breathing, still functioning and still here to help anyone in need through "Four the Boys Foundation" and

F.O.C.U.S. Mark's life, as well as his passing, has affected me tremendously. He continues teaching me how to be a better person. People sometimes ask me if I had it to do all over again, would I have had Mark. My answer is always the same; absolutely. I would never change one second of the twenty years I had with him.

I still wonder, though, about Mark. How would he look today? Would he be married? What would he have named his children? It makes me sad, but the sadness does not take over as it once did. I want my son to be proud of me.

Markie, I am honored to be your mother.

F.O.C.U.S.
Families Of Children United In Spirit
Bereavement Support Group
Flower Hospital
5200 Harroun Road, Sylvania, Ohio 43560
8th Floor, Conference Rooms E & F
7:30 – 9:30 p.m., Fourth Thursday of each month

Four The Boys Foundation
Non-Profit Organization
www.fourtheboysfoundation.com

"LITTLE SUGAR BEAR"

In Memory of Joshua Lucas Berning

By Valrie L. Berning

I'm a single mother of two children. My daughter, Gabrielle, was eight years old when my son, Joshua, was born. I worked the night shift from 7:00 p.m. to 4:00 a.m., Monday through Thursday because it was a full-time position with benefits. I received child support for Gabrielle and Joshua, but their fathers chose not to be active in their lives. My daughter was very mature for her age and didn't want other people coming in to watch them.

Raising two children is a full-time job. Raising a hearing-impaired child is sometimes more than full-time. It never ends. Joshua's father and I split because his addiction to crack was more important. I did not want any of that in my children's lives anymore. I would have to say the most blessed gift God has given us is the ability to create life. Children are a lot of work, but they truly are a joy to watch. They are "miniature entertainers." Both of my children's names are taken from the Bible. I feel God has blessed me well.

April 16, 1993 was the day Joshua came into this world. It was a great joy. Joshua looked and acted like any other newborn. I did not find out until seventeen months later he was profoundly deaf. From birth to seventeen months was a nightmare for me. I'm sure Gabrielle could feel the pressure that I was going through. Working full time, coming home, then getting them ready for the next day was overwhelming. I learned too late to listen to my gut feelings. I let the knowledge of doctors overpower my personal feelings.

Sometimes as parents we get this certain "feeling." It's a feeling we can't let go. We take our child to the doctor who says, "Don't worry, its okay." Sometimes we then question ourselves. Are we too protective? The answer is NO! If you have a nagging feeling, stay with it no matter what even if it's something you don't want to hear. I did this with Joshua. I feel if I didn't have God in my life, I wouldn't have been able to handle all the situations that came my way. I wouldn't have been able to look at the "what ifs" or "he could have been born this way" in a different manner. I also know it could have been worse.

In the beginning, I noticed that Joshua was different from other children when he would sleep. He'd shake, like he was a little disoriented. He would sleep so sound. When I brought this up to my friends, some felt it was normal. Since it had been many years since Gabrielle's birth, I thought it was okay. He was a very happy baby with a very good disposition.

Everyone told me no two babies are alike, even if Gabrielle and Joshua were sister and brother. Trying to remember what Gabrielle did at a certain age was hard. When Joshua was between six and seven months old, I started questioning the doctors. Joshua laughed, smiled back at you, shook rattles, and even walked a little early. He wasn't doing a lot of cooing or babbling. This didn't seem to be a real concern to the doctors.

The insurance company I had dropped my doctor and gave me another doctor that I was unfamiliar with. I made an appointment for Joshua to get his regular check-up. He was thirteen months old. My gut said something was wrong. I told the doctor Joshua made some sounds from time to time, but no words. He told me not to worry, all children are different. I left upset and confused. Again, I questioned myself. Another reason I questioned this doctor was Joshua was due for shots. He said he would have to wait while he looked up Joshua's dosage. In the meantime, Joshua got Chicken Pox. When I took him back to this doctor, he told me I had to return in three weeks for Joshua's shots. The Chicken Pox would be cleared up by then.

Well, I decided to put Joshua through some tests of my own. First, I yelled out his name many times and got no reaction. Joshua also showed no reaction to the phone or sweeper. The only reaction I would get was if I stomped my foot down on the floor. Joshua would look at me. Finally, when Joshua was upstairs in my bedroom with his back to me, I stood in the doorway and screamed "boo" about three times. I snuck up behind him and tapped his little shoulder. He jumped. I knew then and there I was right. I was angry now. I was angry at myself and the doctor. The daycare also told me they felt something was wrong with Joshua. They also thought he couldn't hear. Although I felt pain, I felt relief that I was not the only one who thought this. I was not imaging it. I was a good parent.

When the time came to take Joshua back to the doctor, I told him of my tests and what the daycare said. Finally, the doctor agreed to have Joshua see an ear, nose and throat specialist. At fifteen months, Joshua went to a specialist. He had two tests. The temp-test showed no pressure in his ears. The second was the BEAR test, or brain stem test. Joshua had to be sedated for this. As I waited for the results, I had many thoughts going through my mind. What do I do? Where do I start? I had to get another doctor through my insurance. I finally got the BEAR test results. Joshua's left ear had no hearing and his right ear was 65 decibels and over. I asked the doctor what I should do. His reply was, "Well, speak into his right ear." That was it. He left to see his next patient.

On the way home I thought, "This isn't right. Talk only into his right ear?" It didn't make sense. What had happened to his left ear? I felt the test was wrong. If Joshua could hear with his right ear, why wasn't he acknowledging me and his sister? I made another appointment with a new doctor. This doctor ordered another BEAR test and the results were negative for both ears.

This new doctor took his time with Joshua and checked him thoroughly. The day he was fitted with hearing aids, I came home and cried. I felt numb. I thought of so many things that I had taken for granted. Hearing water, birds chirping, and the snow crunch under my feet. So many thoughts came to mind. I finally stopped, got myself together and thought of how it could be worse. I knew I had to pray, process everything, move forward and just have faith. No matter what, have faith.

I made many phone calls. The audiologist at the hospital enrolled me in the "John Tracey" clinic. I had lessons by mail. It was the best thing that ever happened. Joshua also received home assistance from the county with early intervention for his special needs. The school noted the areas Joshua needed assistance and where he was okay. Sometimes I would catch myself looking at Joshua and wishing he had my hearing. I would ask God at night to give my hearing to him. I had a lot of ups and downs. I knew I had to work with Joshua as he was.

When Joshua got his hearing aids at twenty months old, I don't know what I was thinking. I thought he would be able to talk and hear at the same time. I didn't process that speech and hearing go hand in hand. Joshua's early interventionist came once a week. Gabrielle and I were included with ideas and how to approach Joshua's needs. We also learned how to handle our own frustrations. With Joshua's new hearing aids, I sometimes thought he was doing well and at other times we took two steps back. Joshua was being fitted and tested by a place that did not specialize in children. I didn't know it made a difference, and it was under my insurance plan so I didn't have much input.

Joshua began having inner ear trouble. His inner ear pressure checks could not get a good reading. At two years old, he had tubes put in. Again, I found myself putting my faith in the experts. I would accept their answers to any questions I had about Joshua's audiogram. I got concerned when this audiologist always worried about his money, about the balance which my health insurance would not pay, and when my payments were going to be made. At this time, money was very tight as Joshua's father had left me with large outstanding bills. I told the audiologist not to worry, I would make monthly payments. Stress was taking its toll on me and Gabrielle could see it. I was snappy from working ten hours a day and dealing with Joshua's hearing problems and medical bills.

Finally, when Joshua was a little over two years old, he had a test done with no new results. This was very bad since Joshua should be "gaining" when aided with hearing aids. My parent mentor advised me to get another audiologist. Since my insurance would not cover someone not on my list, I knew I had to make a decision quickly. Each day that Joshua lost, would take another for him to make up. I decided to go outside what my insurance covered. I wanted Joshua to get the best care no matter what the cost. We finally found an audiologist at Flower Hospital who specialized in children. When she first saw Joshua, she noticed his molds were wrong and were blocking the sound he needed. He had lost all that time without hearing.

At 27 months old, Joshua started speech therapy. This was a big adjustment to both Joshua and me. We did total communication with signing. The speech therapist felt something else was wrong with Joshua, but I disagreed.

At this time, Joshua was going to preschool and was still in daycare. I could tell some things were starting to sink in, mainly signing, but Joshua still did not speak except for "mama" once in awhile. By the time he was four and a half, I decided Joshua needed more testing. His teacher thought he might be autistic, so tests were set up at MCO with many different doctors in many fields. All checked Joshua by watching him, asking questions, getting his attention and getting a complete physical check-up. All agreed Joshua did not fit the autistic criteria, but labeled him PDD (Pervasive Developmental Delay) which is a step down from autism. He gets and receives all the information, but doesn't know what to do with it. We knew he could hear with aids, and we now knew what some of his other problems were.

Joshua had an MRI which showed he had a Chart-One. We all produce fluid on our brain, but Joshua produced more and it settled at the base of the brain. For some people this goes unnoticed until late in adulthood when it gets diagnosed from severe headaches, paralysis on one side, etc. I was referred to a brain surgeon who worked with children. The four-week wait to see him seemed like ten years. This was another very stressful time for me and I was depressed.

The brain surgeon apologized to me on behalf of the medical field on how badly we had been treated up to this point. After the exam, he said Joshua essentially had been brain-dead for two and a half years until he had been properly diagnosed and received his hearing aids. Once he could hear, his brain went a little haywire. This explained his mental and physical behavior. He did not recommend surgery since this would be very painful for Joshua.

I decided to take one step at a time. I moved Joshua to a new daycare and eventually to a school that dealt with hearing-impaired children. I took a new job closer to home. Gabrielle was becoming a teenager and with that, had a lot of emotional changes. She wanted to drop out of school to help take care of her brother.

At 15 years old, Gabrielle did drop out of school and got a job. I was not happy with her, but understood why. To make matters worse, she was dabbling in drugs. By this time, I was working full-time in retail, had benefits, but my hours were tricky. I worked Monday through Thursday, 7:00 p.m. to 4:00 a.m. Gabrielle did not want me to get a babysitter for Joshua because he could not defend himself if a sitter did not treat him well. Joshua was not very verbal and we used sign language to communicate. Gabrielle agreed to watch him while I worked since this was easiest for him.

Joshua was a happy boy all the time unless he was sick. His nickname was "Little Sugar Bear" and Gabrielle's was "Sweet Pea." We lived in a three-bedroom condo that I rented from a girlfriend. It was in a nice, close-knit community with about 30 units in a U-shaped area. Joshua and Gabrielle won everyone's hearts and they were loved by our neighborhood. Everyone admired how Gabrielle always looked out for her brother.

My kids were my life. I truly, deeply loved both of them. Gabby would say I loved Joshua more. She never understood there are different levels of love for each child. She would say I babied Joshua because he was deaf. Maybe this was so, but at the time Gabrielle was changing for the worse so fast. I confronted her many times about drugs. She denied using.

I didn't want to push her away, so I left her alone. Everyone would say it's just her age.

Joshua was progressing in school and he had many friends who loved him. He truly was one-of-a-kind. He was getting to a point in his life where he'd become upset with me if I had to pick him up from school for a doctor's appointment because he liked school so much. Eventually, I tried not to do that. I became very involved with the school, teachers and his peers. They were wonderful. Joshua was becoming a little boy who was still behind in some ways but ahead in other ways. Since he was very visual, he could see how something worked and that's all it would take. He would understand it. We would still sign and verbally speak. He'd do the same, maybe not getting all the words right, but he was moving forward.

I was hopeful January, 2002 would be a new year with new beginnings. Joshua was the same happy-go-lucky boy. I was a little stressed and just trying to keep it all together with work and my financial situation. Gabrielle had become tough, distant and short-tempered at me and her brother. I would again question her on using any kind of drugs and the answer was always no. She accused me of picking on her, not trusting her, and being negative so I backed off. Now I know that was the wrong thing to do. Joshua began acting a little strange. He didn't want to be with his sister. He'd sign "piggy" if she were going to watch him. I'd sign "why"? He just could not put it into words. I told Gabrielle I was going to look for a babysitter for him so she could have free time for herself or to be with her friends. She would say no. I told her about the signs from Joshua. She would just say Joshua got angry because she made him clean up messes and that it was just sibling rivalry. Now I wish I would have seen what was really going on.

March, 2002, I got a late call from the police department. They had Gabrielle at the station. She had driven her friends to a store and they got caught stealing liquor. She had her own van she had bought four months earlier, so of course, she had all kinds of friends. I had a friend of mine stay with Joshua while I went to the police station. When I got there, I could tell by looking at Gabrielle she was high. I told the police officer I thought she was high and I wasn't taking her home. He told me she had thrown up several times while she was there, was very irritated, was mouthy and had a nasty disposition. I felt something was very wrong with my daughter, so they called an ambulance and paramedics.

We discovered Gabrielle had taken approximately 34 Coricidin tablets and she had wanted to kill herself. She was admitted to the Psychiatric Unit for three days and given charcoal to get the poison out of her system. Doctors told me that if I hadn't argued with the police at the station, Gabrielle would have fallen asleep and never woke up. Of course I was shocked and wanted her to see a therapist. Gabrielle didn't want any part of it, but did make it to one appointment.

Sunday, March 10, 2002, I went to work and got home around 5:00 a.m. Monday morning. As usual, I went to the basement where Gabrielle's bedroom was to check on the kids. I stayed up until 6:45 a.m. to wake, feed and dress Joshua for school. This particular morning he didn't want to get up, so I called his school and told them he was sick. Gabby went to work around 9:00 a.m. Joshua and I slept in my bed and had a wonderful day together. To this day, I still have the note I wrote for him to be excused. On Monday, March 11, I gave everyone hugs and kisses as usual before I left for work. This time I gave Joshua more than usual and even wrestled him on the floor. For some reason I kept having an uneasy feeling and I thought I'd call home when I got to work. I got busy and before I knew it, I received a phone call around 9:20 p.m. from my neighbor to come home right away. There had been an accident at the condo. I thought, "Okay, everyone's okay."

Then a second call came from someone I thought was my best friend for 16 years. In a very callous voice she said, "Val, I'm not feeling well, but a friend called me and said something about a fire at the condo. Oh yeah, they pulled a body out." I just hung up the phone and you could hear my scream throughout the store.

One of my co-workers and another friend took me to my house. As we were coming up on the street, fire trucks were all over. I got out of the car and ran toward my place. A firefighter grabbed me. As I was fighting to get away and telling him I live here, my daughter approached me. I knew then who was in the fire; my Little Sugar Bear, my Joshua. Firefighters would not let me near Joshua and held me back. As the ambulance pulled out, I could see his little blackened face lying on the cot. I could see he wasn't moving. I tried to run to the back of the ambulance but they held me back again. I could see the lights inside and everyone was working on him. They put me in a police car to go to the burn unit. Soon the ambulance was out of sight, well on their way to the hospital where I thought I would see my son.

It seemed like it took the policeman forever to get to the hospital. As I got out of the car and ran into the ER at St. Vincent's Hospital, I asked for Joshua. I was frantic. The nurses looked at me like I was a crazy woman screaming at them. I insisted on seeing him. They looked at the computer and said, "No such Joshua Berning." By this time I was really screaming, so the nurse in charge decided to call another hospital. She handed me the phone to the trauma doctor at Toledo Hospital. I said to him, "Please tell me the truth about my son's condition. Do not candy-coat anything." His reply, "Ms. Berning, I'm having a very hard time getting your son's heart to beat." I begged him to please keep working on him until I got there. I had been taken to the wrong hospital. I hung up the phone. By this time, Gabrielle and her girlfriend had arrived. I looked at them and told them how selfish they were and they had killed my son. Then I turned to my girlfriend and told her to get me to Toledo Hospital as fast as she could, even it meant running every red light! She did.

I ran through the ER doors of Toledo Hospital, screaming, "Where is my son?" I didn't realize or acknowledge all the police and detectives that were there. They took me to Joshua's room, where nurses were pulling wires and tubes off him. I ordered them to put them back on and to keep working on him. I told them they weren't doing enough, even though inside I knew they had. I looked at my Little Sugar Bear. No life. Blackened skin had just melted away. I held him, I cried, I screamed and who knows what else. I asked everyone to leave the room because I wanted time alone with my son. As any mother would do, I looked at him from top to bottom, hugged him, cried and wondered why. "Lord," I said, "this boy was so innocent and pure."

The ER room was filling up with friends. My boss had closed down the night shift where I worked and brought my co-workers to the hospital. The detectives were coming in trying to ask me questions. They wanted me to go to another room, but I did not want to leave Joshua. I answered what I had to and told them I wanted to be with my son and to please respect that request. What I didn't know at the time was that they were questioning Gabrielle and her friend at the same time, but separately. Two close friends of mine were with my daughter through this process. Gabrielle was then admitted to the Children's Psychiatric Unit because she wanted to kill herself to be with her brother. This is the second story that changed my life and my outlook as well. I would later find out it was just the tip of the iceberg.

I lost my parents some time ago, but when you lose a child words cannot explain the different feelings and emotions that you go through. The saddest and longest night of my life was in that ER room. The hospital staff was trying to comfort me in every possible way. They cut some of Joshua's hair and put it in a flannel bag. They put an angel necklace with his diamond birthstone around my neck. The last thing Joshua and I did was put his little blackened hand in blue tempera paint and put it on canvas. I finally went to my girlfriend's house at about 4:30 a.m. The coroner had to come and take Joshua, which was very hard for me to leave him. I still felt dazed and felt this was all a bad dream. By morning all would be well and normal. It wasn't.

When I woke up the next morning, I knew it was all real. The media had the story splashed all over the news. I wanted to go to the condo to see it. I wanted to feel what had happened. I just had to go. As we pulled into the parking lot, I could see my front porch. There were balloons tied to the porch handle, lit candles, teddy bears and a Detroit baseball hard cap left with a note on it. This touched me so. Then I saw the yellow tape which stated "Crime Scene." I felt such horror. The news media was there. I ran with my two friends to the porch and in through the door as fast as I could. I was not ready to talk to the reporters.

What a mess. Soot all over the floor, the smell of smoke through the entire condo, walls were blackened, and the basement where Joshua passed away. I started to go down the deep, blackened steps that were covered with heavy soot. I looked at the wooden ceiling which was now charred black. I was in such disbelief. Everything was gone or melted. I knew no one could have survived this. As I went back upstairs, I looked at what once was our living room. The wall was axed out by the firefighters, the blinds in the back window were all melted, the back door was busted in from their entrance, and debris was all over the floor. I made my way to the third and final floor of the condo. My room had been axed out and the blinds were melted. I realized the heat had to have been intense and that was why Joshua had suffered thermal burns, not actual fire burns. Then I went into Joshua's room and sat on his bed and cried. I still wanted this to be a bad dream. My friends had to remind me to pick out clothes for Joshua so we could take them to the funeral home. Trying to do that wasn't easy. Looking at all his clothes, I remembered him in each outfit. This would be the final clothing I'd be picking out for my son.

As we all went downstairs, I could hear voices in the living room. A lot of friends and neighbors were there giving me their condolences. At one point, a television crew tried sticking their camera in a hole in the wall to get video of me. One came to the door asking my permission to use the photo they found out back to put it on television. A neighbor told them not to cross the crime scene tape and to leave. Another neighbor told me not to answer them in any way.

It was time for us to leave and get Joshua's clothing to him. As I walked into the funeral home, the director was there to meet me. I asked him if I could see Joshua one more time. He said he didn't think it would be a good idea. Before he could finish, I said, "Nothing could be as bad as what I saw in the ER room. He's my son and I want to hug and kiss him and talk to him for the last time." The funeral director let me into the room. I was not prepared to see what I saw, but I needed Joshua. I needed to be close to him. It was hard to leave. The longer I stayed, the harder it was for me to part from him. I finally did. I had a big day coming up. I had to be there for visitations and the next day for Joshua's funeral.

Walking in for the first time and seeing the closed, little white casket brought out so many emotions in me. It was breathtaking, yet sorrowful. My son loved balloons and the bouquets of them as well as flowers filled the room. Joshua had touched so many people in his short life; people I didn't even know. There was standing room only on the day of the funeral, and the procession was very long. I thought to myself, "Joshua, you touched so many people, you must be a great angel. Do you know what a hole in my heart I have? Do you know how broken it is?"

Gabrielle was out on a pass just for the funeral and had to return to the hospital. I believed that was best for her and because of the feelings going on inside of me. I still felt I was in a dream and none of this was taking place. I was staying at a friend's house and I knew I needed my own space.

I checked into a hotel, which my renter's insurance covered. The aftermath of dealing with everything started settling in. What had happened that night when I left for work? Why did my daughter and her friend leave Joshua alone? My daughter's story was that after I gave everyone hugs and kisses and left for work, she and her friend wanted to get her clothes that she had left at her place. They thought they would be home in a few minutes and thought Joshua would be okay. In reality, that didn't happen. They were gone about 40 minutes. Gabrielle said Joshua was sleeping and thought he would be fine because he never wakes up after he's asleep. She had locked the basement door.

Something in my heart was not setting right. I knew my son inside and out. Gabrielle's story just did not fit.

The first year after Joshua was gone, my daughter put me through hell. She went through a serious crime spree that landed her in CSI. Then she became pregnant. She delivered a boy that looks just like Joshua. It was very bittersweet for me and to this day our relationship is strained. I went to therapy. My daughter then moved out. One year later, I was just beginning to mourn my son's death.

Joshua will live forever inside my heart. In some ways, a large part of me has died. I will never be the same person I was, but through my son and good supportive friends, I am fighting my way back. I want to live again, to laugh, to eat, to smile and to trust. I still go to my son's school. I need the children's love, hugs, and kisses. I need to feel that tapping on my arm when they want my attention or their waving hand in front of my face. Deaf children are more visual and physical. They are all so beautiful.

The day the first school year started without Joshua, I felt so empty. I did not have to buy school supplies. I decided to buy school supplies for children who could not afford them. I call it "Joshua's Box." I told my associates at work what I was doing and they donated as well in memory of Joshua.

During this time, I tried to turn negative thoughts or situations into positive ones. I worked on forgiving the neighbor who heard my son scream the night of the fire and chose to turn up her stereo volume so she couldn't hear him. I forgave Joshua's father who came to the funeral, but never brought flowers or offered to pay any funeral expenses or hospital bills. I was dealing with some of my anger. I knew time was on my side. I also knew that with time, I was getting stronger. When I put Joshua's first-year memoriam in the newspaper, it was very difficult, but it helped at the same time. It was hard for me to think he'd been gone a whole year. It was at this time the final blow came. My daughter told me what really happened the night of the fire.

I had taken Gabrielle out to dinner for her eighteenth birthday. She said, "Mom, I've been holding something inside of me for a long time and I'm not sure if you're really ready to hear this." I told her if it had anything to do with Joshua I'm never ready, but I wanted to know. If it concerned my son, it concerned me. She told me Joshua was awake the night she and her girlfriend had left the condo. I just looked at her. Rage filled inside me. Thankfully, we were out in public. On the way home, all sorts of things went through my mind. Finally when I got home I laid on my bed just thinking, trying to calm down. I called Gabrielle and told her I was sorry. I asked her why she hadn't taken Joshua with her that night. She told me she had left him many times before and he had been okay. I said, "Many? How many?" She told me about ten times. I was hearing all this for the first time. I just couldn't grasp it or her thinking. I said, "Your brother was a special needs child. He needed supervision!" She said, "No, he didn't. You always babied him and I always treated him as if he were eight." I said, "Gabrielle, when you were eight I had a babysitter for both you and your brother. Even though Joshua was eight, mentally he was only about six because of his hearing delay." She just didn't seem to understand.

It's now been five years since the fire. The pain isn't as intense, but I still have my "Joshua Days." Holidays are very tough, as well as his birthday and the anniversary of his death. I think of him everyday. I also know I'm not the same person I was when he was alive. I truly believe that when Joshua died, so did a part of me. It's just something inside of me that has happened. It's like a sore that never heals and just forms a soft scab. Sometimes this scab comes off by a thought or something that I see that reminds me of him. I will always feel that even though I'll move forward in life, I'll have days that I'll go backward. That's okay. A child's death is intense. It's not natural. You never think you'll outlive your child.

I was blessed for eight years and my son taught me three things that take some people a lifetime to learn. Some people may never learn them.

1. *Unconditional love*
2. *Patience*
3. *What it means to really listen (We "hear" but we don't always "listen.)*

Joshua was the best and I will always love him. I will always miss him. I believe I'll see him again. The best advice I can give anyone who has lost a child is to join a group, talk, write, or do anything to get your feelings out. Never hold things in or act like nothing has happened. It will eat at you on the inside. Do what works for you. It may take a lot of time, but healing will come. Stick with what works. I like writing, reading and talking to friends in my FOCUS group. We all share the loss of a child. Without this group, I honestly don't know how I would be today. Today is all I can handle. Tomorrow isn't here and yesterday has passed. So, today is what I have. My prayers will be with anyone who has lost a child. I know your pain.

Acknowledgements:

To my son, Joshua, who was profoundly deaf. With the help of hearing aids, he could hear some things. He showed me what the word "patience" really means.

To my daughter, Gabrielle, who has helped me in many ways. She had a very beautiful bond with her brother.

To our faith in God, who has blessed us by being with us in all our ups and downs. God is number one in our lives.

WHEN GOD CALLS LITTLE CHILDREN

When God calls little children
To dwell with Him above,
We mortals sometimes question
The wisdom of His love.

Perhaps God tires of calling
The aged to His fold,
So he picks a rosebud
Before it grows old.

He knows how we need them
And so He takes but a few
To make the land of heaven
More beautiful to view.

Believing this is difficult
Still somehow we must try.
The saddest word mankind knows
Will always be—Goodbye.

So when a little child departs,
We who are left behind must realize
God, too, loves child—
Angels are hard to find.

DEAF PEACE

Being deaf is a unique thing
You don't hear birds chirp or sing.
Deafness is like blinding darkness,
It's like a death with no sounds heard.
It's like peace with mind together.
We feel vibrations unlike sounds.
God gave us hands and strength to sign.
We have diversified feelings.
Deaf children are like colored rainbows.
We are ordinary people,
We think like you,
We laugh and cry,
We have insecurity,
But in our culture,
We feel free.

AUTUMN RAIN

Do not stand at my grave and weep.
I am not there, I do not sleep.
I am a thousand winds that blow,
I am the diamond glints upon the snow.
I am the sunlight on ripened grain,
I am the gentle autumn rain.
When you awaken in the morning's hush,
I am that swift uplifting rush,
Of quiet birds in circled flight.
I am the soft star that shines at night.
Do not stand at my grave and cry,
I am not there.
I did not die.

CHRISTMAS

I see the countless Christmas trees around the world below
With tiny lights, like heaven's stars, reflecting on the snow.
The sight is so spectacular, please wipe away that tear
For I am spending Christmas with Jesus Christ this year.

I hear the many Christmas songs that people hold so dear
But the sounds of music can't compare with the Christmas
choir up here.
I have no words to tell you the joy their voices bring
For it is beyond description to hear the angels sing.

I know how much you miss me; I see the pain inside your
heart
But I am not so far away, we really aren't apart.
So be happy for me, dear ones, you know I hold you dear
And be glad I'm spending Christmas with Jesus Christ this
year.

I send you each a special gift from my heavenly home above
I send you each a memory of my undying love.
After all, "Love" is the gift more precious than pure gold
It was always most important in the stories Jesus told.

Please love and keep each other, as our Father said to do
For I can't count the blessings or love he has for you.
So, have a Merry Christmas and wipe away the tear
Remember, I'm spending Christmas with Jesus Christ this
year.

FAVORITE SONGS

"Calling All Angels" (by Train)
"When I Look To The Sky" (by Train)
"Heaven" (by Los Lonely Boys)
"Blurry" (by Puddle of Mud)
"My Immortal" (by Evanescence)

I'M PROUD OF YOU

In Loving Memory Of Nick

By Angela Christensen

"Thank you! Enjoy your day!" I say as I give my customer her change and put her receipt and a copy of our store flyer in her bag. My eyes glance at the flyer. Each customer receives a list of our products with an explanation for the purpose of our store. "July 19, 2001" jumps out at me. Has it really been eight years?

July 19, 2001 is the day my life as I knew it ended. It is the day my oldest child, Nick, was killed in an auto accident while running an errand for work. He was 19 years old. Even now, recalling that day quickens my heartbeat, brings stabbing pain in my chest, sickens my stomach, and weakens my entire body. I still have a difficult time believing I am now living this life—a life without one of my children.

Eight years. I take a few moments from my busy schedule to reflect, to try to remember. Who was I before July 19, 2001? Where is that person who was so innocent, so naïve, so unaware of what life had in store for me? I can barely bring those memories to the surface. Buried deep where my old self used to inhabit, I recall my "blissfully ignorant" life. I had simple goals, quiet aspirations, and a clear vision of my future.

I was married to my high school sweetheart, Mark. We had built a life in rural Michigan with our three children, Nick, Eric and Amanda. I had fulfilled my dream of being a mom and living in the country. We were a typical American family working hard to give ourselves and our children a good life. I felt my job was to prepare Nick, Eric and Amanda for adulthood. I wanted to see them grow up and make a life for themselves. Mark and I would share their ups and downs as they raised their own families. We would reap the benefits of hard work by enjoying our grandchildren. It was a simple plan.

Thursday, July 19, 2001 began like so many other mornings. It was just after 6:00 a.m. and I awoke to Nick's loud alarm. Because he was such a sound sleeper, Nick would sometimes not hear his alarm and I would have to go upstairs to wake him for work. I went to his bedroom door and saw him in bed. From the doorway, I asked if he was awake and teased him by asking if he wanted me to come in there to wake him up. He smiled and said, "Yeah, Mom, you come in here and wake me!" I laughed and went back to bed knowing he was fully awake. I heard him in the kitchen, heard the kitchen door shut, and then heard his truck pull out of the driveway like I had dozens of times before.

As I had done countless other mornings in my life, an hour later I got up and got ready for my day. It was beautiful, sunny and hot outside. My morning started with thoughts about supper and what chores needed to be done around the house. I arrived at my job around 9.00 a.m. I was a professional wallpaper hanger, and I hung blue wallpaper in a bathroom. I left about 3:30 p.m., stopped at a garage sale, went home briefly and talked to Amanda while she was washing her car. I went on to the grocery store and bought what I needed to make supper. I was just leaving the store parking lot when my cell phone rang. It was Amanda. She was crying. Instantly alarmed, my heart started beating fast when she asked me where I was. I told her I was just leaving the grocery store, and asked her what was wrong. She said, "Come home, Mom." I again asked her what was wrong. All she would say was, "Just come home, Mom."

I hung up the phone and sped out of the parking lot. The five-mile drive home seemed like an eternity. Everything was in slow motion. I thought something had happened to our dog, Ivan, whom we love deeply. I knew Mark, Nick and Eric were at their jobs until 5:00. Amanda was home washing her car. Everyone in my mind was accounted for. By this time, it was about 4:30 p.m.

As I turned into our driveway and approached the house, I saw Mark, Eric, and Amanda coming down the porch steps. They were all crying uncontrollably. As I got out of my van, I knew. I knew. I knew. One person wasn't there. Nick. Amanda walked up to me. She could barely speak through her sobs, saying, "Nick was killed in a car accident." I collapsed onto the lawn. Nothing was real. I heard screams coming from me, my chest was heaving and my heart was pounding. My body was heavy and my legs wouldn't work. Mark picked me up and helped me into the house. I was hugging Eric and Amanda, while clinging to Mark. I remember his chest heaving with deep sobs. In the kitchen, I fell onto the floor. Time literally stood still.

This cannot be happening. This cannot be real. Over and over I asked, "How can we go on, how can we go on?" I was no longer in this world. I was instantly zapped into another reality that was a nightmare. My mind could not register what was happening. My heart could not understand that one of my children was gone forever.

Mark and Amanda then told me how two police officers from the Michigan State Police Department came to our home and saw Amanda outside washing her car. They asked her where her parents were, and told her to call them to come home. They went on to tell her that Nick died at 12:40 p.m. in an auto accident. He had gone left of center while running an errand for work. He hit an asphalt truck head on. He had died instantly. The driver of the asphalt truck was taken to the hospital with only minor injuries. The officers gave Amanda their telephone numbers and left. At 16 years of age, she had the responsibility of calling Mark, Eric and me to give us the awful news.

In shock, Mark and I decided to tell our parents in person. Because of their ages and health, we tried to stay as composed as possible. It was pure hell. I felt like a little girl wanting my Mom and Dad to hold me in their arms and tell me everything would be all right. I wanted this to be a bad dream. I wanted to go back to yesterday. I wanted my old life back. Of course, none of this happened. My life was forever changed. I would never be "all right" again.

News spread quickly about Nick's death and dozens of friends and family members came to our house. I couldn't tell you who was there or what was said. Everything was a blur. Friends, brothers, sisters, and neighbors came through our door with wild-eyed looks of horror on their faces. There were questions, hugs, words and endless tears. The rooms of my dear old farmhouse became heavy with sadness, horror and grief.

At some point that evening, we decided to go to the hospital morgue. I knew if I did not see Nick's body, I would have a difficult time believing he was gone for the rest of my life. Mark, Eric, Amanda, my nephew, Phil, and our dog, Ivan, rode in our van in silence. At the hospital, we were escorted to a room where a nurse spoke to us about what to expect when we saw Nick. She explained the extent of his injuries.

I told her Nick wished to be an organ donor, so she assured us his corneas and bones would be used. We would later learn Nick's donation never took place. No paperwork had been filed. I wanted to have Nick's beautiful blue eyes help someone to see, but my hope that at lease a small part of Nick would live on was crushed. As we entered our new life, this was my first of many encounters with insensitive people.

Two nurses escorted us down a long hall. They wiped tears from their eyes when opening the door to the morgue. We walked in, not prepared for what we were about to see. No parent should ever have to experience their child lying lifeless on a table in a cold, sterile morgue. Nick looked as if he were sleeping. He was pale and had a deep gash over his left eye. His body was covered with a blanket from the chest down. He still had his clothes, shoes and chain necklace on. The nurses told us he had severe trauma to his chest and to the back of his head. His lower body was crushed and the "Jaws of Life" had been used to remove him from his truck.

Amanda and I walked up first, followed by Phil, Eric and Mark. I stroked Nick's cheek and laid my hand on his upper chest. There was no heartbeat. He was so cold. I had felt his face just two days before while cutting his hair. I knew what my eyes were seeing, but I could not comprehend it. This was the beautiful body my energetic son had been in just hours before. Now it was a cold, empty, lifeless shell. Where was my Nick? Where was his boundless energy?

One by one, Amanda, Eric, Phil and Mark all said their final good-byes to Nick. We were all sobbing and holding each other up. We left the morgue and I walked the long hospital hallway arm-in-arm with Amanda. I wondered how my legs were working without my heart. Walking, talking, thinking—things I had done everyday of my life were now cumbersome and not connected to "me." The "me" from a few hours before was gone. I was now functioning in some kind of hellish "other-world."

I sat numb on the ride home. I didn't know where I was, but I knew I was not in the world that I saw whizzing by the van windows. By this time it was dark and stars were appearing. I kept wondering where Nick was. What was he doing now? Seeing his body made his physical death real.

Arriving home, someone told us to watch the news at 11:00 p.m. Nick's accident was the top story. We watched in horror as we saw the accident scene, Nick's beautiful red pickup truck in a mangled mess, and our son in a body bag on a gurney being wheeled into an ambulance. This footage would play for the next couple days and people would repeatedly ask us if we had seen it. It sickens me to this day to think of those images on television. Why did people think this was something we needed to see? Compounding our pain, the news station called repeatedly asking for an interview. They wanted a segment on the "family's reaction" to Nick's death. Thankfully, friends and relatives intercepted these telephone calls and told reporters to leave us alone.

The next few days were a blur of non-stop people coming to our home. Even in the darkness of my grief, I was touched by the kindness and thoughtfulness of others. Mark and I sat on our couch in the living room accepting countless visitors from every aspect of our lives, answering the same questions over and over, barely clinging to our sanity – barely clinging to life. Friends and family organized food, stocked coolers of drinks, did our laundry, answered the telephone, and collected pictures of Nick for the funeral.

I felt a spiritual closeness to Mark that's difficult to describe. It still lingers today. On the day Nick was born, Mark and I shared a bond in the miracle of being a part of creating his new life. Now we were at the opposite end of the spectrum sharing the unimaginable pain of his death. We knew we were the two people who loved him most, so his death would affect us the most.

The day after Nick's accident, we went to the funeral home to make arrangements. We both remembered a conversation we had with Nick just the year before. After coming home from my 90-year-old grandmother's funeral, Nick was agitated about the whole funeral process. He told us he wanted to be cremated and he didn't want his body shown. He said people should be happy when someone dies because they would be in heaven and in a better place. He went on to say he wanted to be remembered in life, not death, and that he wanted a party in his memory. Of course we were shocked Nick had such specific opinions on funeral plans, and we teasingly told him he would be burying us. Needless to say, after that conversation, Mark and I wanted to honor Nick's wishes.

Sunday, July 22, 2001 we woke up to day four of our new nightmare and, like robots, dressed for Nick's funeral. On our drive into town, I remember looking out at all the people in their yards wishing I could trade places with them. Just before we got to the funeral home, Mark put his hand over mine and said, "If 19 years ago I had a choice whether to have Nick or not—knowing he would die young, would I choose not to have him, to avoid this pain, or would I choose to experience Nick, I would do it all again. Knowing Nick for 19 short years was worth the pain of losing him." I couldn't have agreed more.

We had a closed casket with Nick's graduation picture on top and we played his favorite songs and showed pictures and a video of his life. Eric wore Nick's favorite soccer shirt and at 17 years old, gave a beautiful eulogy for his brother. At the end of the day, Nick's friends played the CD of their favorite song called "Dammit" by Blink 182. It was a one-day visitation, and over 1,000 people attended. I don't remember what people said that day, what the minister talked about, or who was there. I only knew my heart was broken and I would never recover. Nick was later cremated.

Six weeks after the funeral, we had a bonfire at our house just as Nick had done dozens of times before with his friends. This time would be different. The party was to honor and remember Nick's life. We used Nick's last paycheck to buy pizza and drinks, and we told everyone the party was on Nick. More than 50 close friends of Nick's showed up and stayed into the early morning hours reminiscing, crying and laughing. Even though this was an extremely difficult party for Mark and me, it was truly cathartic. We knew we had honored Nick's wishes. We knew he would be proud of us.

We buried Nick's ashes a few weeks later in a very small, historic cemetery about a mile from our house. It would take us four years to have a headstone made and installed. We just did not have the strength to see Nick's name in stone on his gravesite. To this day, I do not connect Nick to the cemetery. It is just a place to mark his physical life on this earth.

In the days and weeks following Nick's death, time went by slowly. One never-ending day blended into the next and the pain was excruciating. Just thinking of Nick, hearing certain songs, the mention of his name, anything related to my loss—all were like sucker punches to my stomach or a knife piercing my heart. I never knew a person could cry so much. I drank a lot of water because I was so dehydrated. I remember looking in the mirror at a stranger with swollen eyes and a gaunt face. I just wanted to sleep. I wanted to escape the hell I was in. I had no hope and no will to live.

Basically, I spent the first months after Nick's accident in bed or on our couch. I truly knew how someone could take her own life. I was 44 years old and could easily have to live 44 more years with this loss. How was I supposed to go on? I couldn't work or eat and lost 25 pounds. I was physically sick and weak with no desire to wear makeup or dress nicely. My hands shook constantly. I couldn't concentrate or even think, and for months had anxiety attacks and paranoia. I was constantly "zoning out" while in the middle of something and had flashbacks of the morgue, the accident, the funeral and Nick's face. I would drive somewhere and not remember how I had gotten there.

I was diagnosed with "post-traumatic stress" and my doctor prescribed an anti-depressant. It didn't help. Everyone seemed to look at me with either pity or fear; many treated me like a leper. They didn't want to get too close for fear of "catching" what I had, or they just didn't know what to say. In our community, Mark and I were now "the couple who lost their son."

By far, the most hurtful reactions to our loss were the comments and judgments of some of the people who were closest to me. Because I had been raised Catholic and had chosen not to raise my children so, I was highly criticized. I was even told Nick could not be in heaven. Some people just could not believe an auto "accident" could happen. They were sure drugs or alcohol had been a factor. They were convinced we were covering something up. I was even told Nick had been an embarrassment to the family.

Even to this day, I cannot put into words the pain I still feel from these remarks. It didn't matter that I was at the lowest point I would ever be in my life. Apparently, I was open game for people to criticize and judge me because I was such an irresponsible parent that my child was killed. This was somehow my "punishment."

When I lost my child, my world came to an end. It was very hard for me to understand how the world around me could just keep on spinning. Time had not stood still for everyone else as it had for me. People resumed their "normal" lives and thought I should too. I not only missed Nick terribly, but every single aspect of my life was now different.

Everyday life is a challenge that brings new heartaches, new tears and new decisions to make. The dynamics of our family has changed for all of us. How do I answer people's questions about how many children I have? How do I sign birthday and Christmas cards? What should I do with the mail addressed to Nick? How do I deal with the empty seat at the dinner table? How can I go grocery shopping without breaking down when I see the food I would buy for Nick? What should I do with Nick's clothes, his room, and his possessions?

I have worried endlessly how Nick's death will affect Eric and Amanda. They have had to deal with the enormity of the sudden loss of their brother. Mark and I could not be there for them as well as we should have because we were so overwhelmed with our own grief. I'm sure they did not want to come to us with their feelings because they did not want to upset us or see us cry more. I think Eric and Amanda do not relate well to others their own age now. They have met death and have lost their innocence. I feel they are deeper and wiser than most adults.

To compound our loss, within six months of losing Nick, Mark lost his job and a business partnership. This also meant we lost our retirement along with thousands of dollars on a business investment. Mark and I felt defeated by life.

Throughout my life, I have been an avid reader. Of special interest to me are books on angels, the after-life, near-death experiences and anything spiritual. I have also been drawn to like-minded people for discussions on these topics. I feel I've been on a spiritual quest my entire adult life. I have always felt there was so much more than what I had learned in my catechism class. I now feel I was led to read these books and to meet these people to gain the insight I needed to prepare me for the loss of my son. I know I would not have gotten through the days, weeks and months after Nick's death without these spiritual beliefs.

I wanted our children to be open-minded. I wanted them to know they are divine, spiritual beings experiencing a physical life. I think we as a society are only just beginning to realize the magnitude of our spirit. I also believe we live many physical lives. It only makes sense to me that we could not possibly learn all we must learn in one lifetime. During their growing years, Nick, Eric and Amanda were exposed to traditional and non-traditional spiritual views and we had many such discussions.

In the days immediately following Nick's death, I knew he was still spiritually with us. I never blamed God. I believed these were lessons I chose before birth to learn, as difficult as they seem on an earthly level. As I looked back at Nick's life, how energetic he was and how he lived life so fully, I knew he had an inner-knowing that his life would be short. After his funeral, a few of his friends told me Nick said he couldn't see himself living past the age of 22. He knew.

I've had many dreams of Nick that I would call visitations. We cry, we hug, and we tell each other "I love you." It is very real and colorful. Whenever I have one of these dreams, I am deeply affected. I know Nick has visited me. I have had other numerous communications from Nick. Light bulbs have burst when I walked by, pictures of Nick have fallen over, birds and butterflies come unusually close and flutter, and I've had small prisms of light appear out of nowhere in my house and reflect on my body. I know I get messages from Nick through music, especially when his favorite songs come on the radio at the times when I miss him the most. I even think our dog, Ivan, has had visits from Nick. I've seen Ivan run and play in the yard in a way he only did with Nick. When that happens, I don't think Ivan is alone.

I have discovered people can be divided into two basic groups when it comes to loss. Those who have experienced the death of a close loved one, especially their child, are more open to after-death communication. Then there are those who have not experienced a loss.

Once someone discovers that I have lost my son, they are very open and tell me many stories about their after-death communication and visitations. It is as if they are disclosing a deep, dark secret they know only "people like us" will understand. I feel bereaved people have been given a gift from their loved ones in the next world. The non-bereaved person only views these "visitations" with their worldly eyes, and sees them as a self-made coping mechanism for grief.

After Nick died, I visited several local spiritual mediums. It makes sense to me that some people can be gifted in a sensory way where they can receive feelings and messages from the next world. Several of these messages brought me comfort. It was not until August, 2002 that I truly felt our physical world and Nick's spiritual world met. This happened when Mark and I went to New York City to visit George Anderson.

I read George Anderson's books in the months after Nick's death. They brought me hope when I had none. They gave me understanding and the strength to go on in my life. I hung the following paragraph from George Anderson's book "We Don't Die" on my refrigerator where I could read it daily.

"Everything that happens in your life has a purpose. There is no one you are close to who ever dies. Everyone just goes on to another stage of life that runs parallel to this one. Be at peace with yourself and fulfill your mission here, knowing that your stay here is temporary, and that you are doing something here to fulfill your spiritual purpose. Tune in more to yourself. And understand more within yourself so that you can find your way easier. Don't place so much emphasis on life materially, place more emphasis on it spiritually. There is no such thing as death. That child, that husband, that wife, that loved one—they are all still very much alive."

I decided I wanted a session with George Anderson. Through a series of "coincidences" and pure belief that Nick wanted us to meet, Mark and I found ourselves driving to New York City one year after Nick's death. Against the odds, we had somehow gotten an appointment with George Anderson. Mark was going as a skeptic, but would come home a believer. I was absolutely positive Nick had set this up for us.

I cannot put into words how accurate George Anderson's information was and how healing his words were. We received very personal messages that astound us to this day. Mark and I are convinced Nick spoke directly to us through

George. We walked away with a clearer understanding of our physical life, our spiritual life, and our son's life in the next world. I feel meeting with George Anderson was Nick's gift to us. It brought some measure of comfort in our darkest days of overwhelming grief.

As the weeks and months ticked by, Mark and I slowly adjusted back to the earthly world. We knew we were forever changed. Mark opened his own collision business and I began taking on occasional wallpaper jobs. All those little things in life that used to be so important were now very unimportant. The goals and aspirations we had for ourselves were memories. The thrill of life was gone.

The only shred of life I had left was the love I had for Eric, Amanda and Mark. The four of us now had an unspoken bond, an inner knowing that we had experienced a spiritual connection few ever will. We were trying to survive the unpredictable waters of life by floating on a thin, shaky raft; clinging to each other, each being tempted to go under to drown the pain. We all came to the same conclusion—love was all that mattered. Love kept us afloat.

Within two years, Amanda went off to college. Eric found a job, bought a house, and moved out. Mark and I became empty-nesters. Our once hectic, noisy, teenager-filled home was now silent. But our sorrow and the changes in our life brought us closer together.

To our friends and family, I'm sure I seemed to be getting "better." I knew everyone who loved me just wanted me to be happy again. They had no concept of the permanent damage that was done to my heart and soul. Nick's death had been a cataclysmic event that had altered my life forever. I learned to put on my happy face and pretend to fit back into my old lifestyle. Mark and I know we have to continue on in this world and want to maintain the wonderful friendships we have, but I have come home countless times only to cry myself to sleep. I just don't fit in anymore. I am different.

After Nick's death, it didn't take long for me to figure out that only other parents who had lost a child would truly understand what I was going through. No matter how well-intentioned or professionally trained someone may be, if they haven't experienced the loss of their child, they don't have a clue. An acquaintance I barely knew, who had lost her son eight months before I lost Nick, contacted me. Five weeks after Nick's passing, she invited me to come with her to a bereavement group called F.O.C.U.S.—Families Of Children United in Spirit. It would be a turning point in my healing.

At my first meeting, my grief was too deep to comprehend how all these people at the meeting could be talking and even smiling. The women even had make-up on. How could this be? With time, I understood. At first, I went intermittently to the monthly meetings. Grief was very hard work. After a while, I started going to most monthly meetings. I found friendships, confidantes, and hope in these parents who had suffered the ultimate loss. With each heartbreaking story and with every shared emotion, I grew. I was not alone anymore. I became stronger, wiser and more hopeful about my new life. With the years, I became more involved and eventually realized I was helping the newly bereaved. Somewhere along the line when I was searching for help, I began helping others. F.O.C.U.S. was a lifeline that pulled me back to the land of the living.

Sometime during the third year after Nick's passing, I came up with the idea of opening an angel-specialty gift store. I had never owned a retail business before, but I just knew I wanted to do something meaningful and to help others. I have always been drawn to angels because they gave me hope and comfort. In fact, Nick's last gift to me was an angel garden statue. A close friend, who had lost her daughter, thought a store would be a nice way to honor Nick.

With this vague concept in my head, I started looking at storefront properties. I really didn't have a clue what I had to do, but I was confident my angels and Nick were guiding me. That once-vague concept grew into an all-consuming thought. After six months of searching, Mark and I purchased a beautiful old building in the downtown historic block of Sylvania, Ohio. It is a five-minute drive from our home. The century-old building had been a home, then a dentist's office, and would now become Angela's Angels & Antiques gift shop.

In the beginning, I thought I would be doing something positive to help others. Surprisingly, I found out that every aspect of owning our store was helping me. I have absolutely no doubt in my mind that I was led to do what I am doing today. The events occurred in perfect sequence: for us to own a property that was not for sale, find a bank that would finance our venture, and have another angel store owner in another state help us. These were not coincidences! Even though I had no experience in retail, in my mind I had nothing to lose. I had survived the ultimate loss, so the possibility of a failed business venture was minor. I just knew everything I had done previously in my life had prepared me for this. Now with my knowledge of grief and loss, I could fill a need.

Angela's Angels & Antiques opened in November, 2004. Our gift shop specializes in angels of all kinds for the home and garden. About half our sales involve bereavement and comfort items. We sell and deliver funeral and memorial gifts. We carry books on angels, grief, and spirituality. I felt what had helped me early in my grief could help others, as well.

Daily I hear heartbreaking stories of illness and loss, and I know I am in the right place at the right time for this person. I also meet extremely positive and spiritual people who inspire me. I now work with psychics, mediums, light workers, healers, and energy workers. Like a sponge, I am absorbing new spiritual knowledge.

From the avid angel collector to the person searching for a comfort gift, our angel merchandise conveys unspoken messages of hope, love and happiness. I know my angels and Nick have led me on this journey to find peace. In so doing, I now help others with their grief. I am where I should be right now in my life. When I tell each customer, "Enjoy your day," I truly mean it. Each day is a blessing—a chance to learn and grow.

Even though I firmly believe Nick is closer to me in spirit than I can ever imagine, I miss his physical presence. I often wonder what he would be doing today. What would he look like now? What would he be doing with his life? I try to picture his face, but the details are getting foggy with time. Many of his friends are married and have children. Two babies have been named after him. It hurts to know we will never experience Nick's own children. We will never know what kind of grown man, husband and father he would have been. Would all of our love, guidance and hard work as parents have paid off?

Every morning, I take a walk with our dogs. This is my time to pray, talk to Nick, and speak to my angels and spirit guides. I ask for guidance and inspiration. I ask for help in my daily life and in the lives of friends and family. I also give thanks for all my blessings. I look back at my life and realize how far I've come. Many days are still very difficult, but I make a conscious effort to think positive. I have learned to let go and forgive.

As I look back, my life's journey has been divided into two distinct parts. There was my naive life before Nick passed and my profound life after. In my early grief, I wanted my old life back. It would take me years to realize that would never happen. That person, that life is gone forever. I have grown lifetimes in eight short years. I also know I still have so much to learn. I believe Mark, Nick, Eric, Amanda and I entered into this lifetime with the agreement that Nick would pass at a young age. This was his gift to us for our spiritual growth.

I used to worry how I could live another 44 years with the pain of this loss. Now I look forward to old age with Mark and sharing my life with Eric and Amanda and, hopefully, their families someday. I take one day at a time, knowing my earthly life will be over in the blink of an eye. I focus on helping others through my experience. I want to be the best person I can be until I cross over to the next world. I have absolutely no fear and look forward to my own death when that time comes. I know Nick will be the first to greet me on the other side. I cannot wait for our reunion. My hope is for Nick to say, "I'm proud of you, Mom."

Angela's Angels & Antiques
5774 Main Street
Sylvania, Ohio 43560
(419) 824-4079
www.angelasangelsgifts.com

THEY LEFT

A Brother's Story

By Eric Christensen

I awoke hearing loud voices downstairs. Someone was yelling. Rolling over I guessed it was somewhere around 11:00 in the morning. To a seventeen year-old in the summer before his senior year of high school, that was early. At this time in my life, how early I had to wake up was one of my biggest concerns. I didn't have a full-time job, didn't have a girlfriend, and didn't really have a life. I just lived day-to-day. I had no worries.

Again, I heard the loud voices. It was time to get up; time to see who was picking on my little sister this time. I had a good guess as to who it was. I stumbled downstairs to a typical setting. Nick, my older brother who had graduated from high school, was home from work on his lunch break. As usual, he was one of the voices I had heard shouting in the kitchen. On the receiving end was "little" Amanda, my sixteen year-old baby sister. She was sitting at the island counter taking the verbal abuse her older brother threw in her direction. Entering in the midst of their debate, I pieced some of the conversation together. Nick believed that the Backstreet Boys were not much of a musical talent, while the band Blink 182 was infinitely better. He had just been to their concert the night before.

As I entered, Nick spotted me and made a quick lunge in my direction to connect a fair shove to let me know I was awake. Sadly, for Amanda and me, picking on us and playful punches were Nick's ways of saying, "Top of the morning to ya!" Since the day had just begun, the mood was light and nice. After a few more "nasty" comments about Amanda's music choices, another hard push into my shoulder, and comments about us sleeping while he was busy working, Nick headed to the door. He looked us both in the eye and said "good-bye" as he strode out with his heavy gait. The day went on.

With our parents both working their lives away, I decided to drive a few miles into town to pass the day. I finished my pointless duties and returned home a few hours later. When I approached our driveway, I noticed a Michigan State Trooper cruiser in our yard. I thought to myself that my little sister must have gotten pulled over. This was not unusual since there would be speed traps up the road from time to time. I smiled thinking that the police officers were scaring her into a safe driving habit. Or maybe they would just give her a ticket and she would learn early to keep the speed down.

I exited my vehicle to find no officers outside anywhere, so I began to walk to the house. As I reached the front door, I could clearly see Amanda in full tears. Once again, I just thought this was a normal reaction to getting a speeding ticket. Before I had full footing inside the kitchen door, two state troopers greeted me. Both had their hats off; a man and a woman. The woman had dark hair and struck me as being strong as she stood with a means and had a point to make. She asked who I was and if Nicholas was my brother. Of course he was my nineteen year-old, massively artistic, spiky-haired, shorter brother! She continued to tell me that he had been in an auto accident and lost his life on impact.

There I stood. I was no longer partially in my parent's kitchen with two state troopers and a weeping sibling. I entered a void. I couldn't feel; not just my body, but my being. I wasn't there. I didn't just lose my only brother that could not be the truth! Stepping momentarily from the mental darkness, I asked the state trooper if she were sure. She just nodded. The strength it took her to do her job was beyond me.

I don't know how much time passed, it had to be only minutes, but it seemed like years. Life faded away. A mission was created in my head. I had to find out if this was the truth. I needed to get the troopers out. Within moments, Dad arrived. Apparently, Amanda had phoned him. Thinking just a short time ago that he was a father of three, now he had to continue in this life with only two. I still cannot imagine how he didn't come undone right then and there.

The state troopers talked to my dad, but I went back into the gray void. Again, time stopped. Finally, the troopers were on their way. I assume they would look at their lives in a different light, possibly to love what they have just a little more than just the day before. I knew at that moment my life had changed forever. The life I had for the past seventeen years had been all about me; one day to the next, just me. No more.

Mom pulled into the driveway. She didn't know what had happened only that something was horribly wrong. Amanda wanted to tell her; even though she could hardly talk. As she greeted Mom in the yard with the news, Mom fell to her knees just a few steps from the car. To bring a life into the world only to have it taken away from her had taken a major toll. To see this woman who ushered me into the world come undone is a sight that killed a deep part of my youth. I don't remember crying, probably because that is all I did. I guess crying became a reflex, like breathing. Our family of five turned upside down into a house of four lost beings. I had taken my life as I knew it for granted.

I decided I had to tell a few close family members in person. The first was my brother-like cousin, Phil. I went to his house and I walked up to him as he was washing his truck. He stopped dead in his tracks once he heard the news. Never a man of many words he had nothing to say, but his eyes spoke louder than any words could. I drove from house to house spreading the darkness over our tiny town. Each person I told reacted to the harsh truth differently. Some couldn't believe what they were hearing. Some felt it deep down; it was the truth. Others just shut down. We all died a little that day.

A little more life returned to me after telling each family member or friend of Nick's death. It was almost like it grounded me to see this as a truth; not a dream. This sick way of coping was only the beginning of the pain. After my rounds, I returned home where every sight in the house was a constant reminder of my new agony. Seeing old memories and knowing that there wouldn't be new ones. It was a strange feeling—to call the only home I had ever known a prison, but that is what it had become.

I managed to get phone numbers to find out where Nick was for the time being. My family reached an agreement to see Nick for one last time. That night, as a family, Dad, Mom, Amanda, Phil and I packed into the van for a dark trip. The drive was long. I've never known 45 minutes to last years like it did that night. I saw other people driving along the same road and it made me jealous to see others living their happy lives. They had no problems. They were just going home for the evening to their perfect family and perfect life. Why was this happening to us? We never did anything wrong! Why was this evil pain coming down on such a good group of people? This feeling faded as I drifted in and out of darkness.

Finally we were at our destination, the hospital. It was late. I felt like I was in a scene from a movie. Despite it being summer, I was cold. A woman came out and asked if we were sure this was what we wanted then she led us back to the morgue. Like a dream that haunts you from the depths of your subconscious, we all acquired a very real image of death. Pale and cold is the only way to describe the sight. We could finally believe what we had been told—it solved nothing. That would be my motto for some time to come—every solution I came up with for my problems and depression solved nothing.

As the next few days crept by, a "sticky" feeling held me back from being emotionally there. It was a trial everyday to wake and find myself living the same nightmare. I tried to be strong, tried to hold myself together—not for myself, but for my family. We needed each other. Whether we liked it or not, we were stuck together sharing this same issue. Growing up, my parents were the rigid backing of my life. They were the solid support that let me know everything would be okay. When I lost that footing, I felt the weight got transferred onto me. To see my parents, the undisputed rulers in my life, break down made me have a hard time not to do the same. The pain they had to endure goes beyond my understanding. To see into the eyes of true pain made me lose hope. In the end, I had to find out who I was and let that person take control. Then life would go on.

Some people I counted as great friends showed their true colors in my time of need and were not true friends at all. Other people I really wanted help from, but their lives came first, not mine. Some people were even so cruel as to think they could get attention for themselves by acting like my friend. I have held much of this against certain friends and it took years to let that go. Some people came out of nowhere and surprised me in unexpected ways, while others came to me with fear at how I would react and tried—for me.

I can think of several people (outside of my mom, dad and sister) who were there for me. One was a family member. A bond formed that I doubt will ever die, because there was a day he felt my pain and I felt his. From that day, we made a wordless vow to let Nick live through us merely by how he picked on us. That was Nick's way of showing us affection. We both call each other by a silly nickname my brother once used.

There were also two brothers who took an evening off their busy lives to come to me. Avoiding the large crowd that plagued our house for several days after Nick's accident, the brothers chose the cover of night to pay a visit with just hugs and a few simple words, "I'm sorry." This simple act, coming from them in this situation meant the world to me.

Also there for me, was a life-long friend who never ran from anything. He is a true man, and if I ever had a hero he would be one of them. I eluded the mob of strangers that camped around our house because I needed to get away, but I didn't want to be alone. Retreating to my high school football field for sanctuary, I found a suitable spot to call mine. He arrived. We both sat in silence as a swarm of mosquitoes took their toll. It seemed like we sat for hours. I knew I needed this, but he could have been anywhere else doing any number of better things. I am really thankful for that.

A young lady I hadn't spoken with for some time came to the funeral. My family and I had been there all day. The horde of people that showed up sucked the energy right out of all of us. I was tired and sick of being around so many people. This young lady marched through the buzzing crowd with purpose to find me. She grabbed my hand, looked me in the eyes and must have read my mind. She dragged me out of the building into the fresh air and never let go of my hand. She was driven to help. It worked for that moment.

These are such small things to do when something so bad happens. These "small things" will always push me to put myself aside and think of others like these people had done for me. I now know other people who have lost a family member and regardless if I think that person is struggling, I feel they need to know I care. I write a note, give them a call or drop in and let them know how I feel. I will put aside my fear of how they might react because in these situations it is about them, not me. I learned this from my friends when Nick died. In the chaos of this type of horror, it's hard to predict a person's actions.

With time, life got harder. Meeting new people would inevitably involve a simple question. "So, do you have any brothers or sisters?" How do you answer that? "No, I don't have a brother in the physical sense. I had a brother once and he died, but his influence on my life lives through me!" So, at the age of seventeen going on thirty-five, I kept it simple. The answer is, "Yes, I have one younger sister." I just didn't like the way people looked at me when I told them the truth; a blank stare while their lips slowly split with the words, "Oh, I'm so sorry to hear that." This seemed like a good answer. I went on with my life trying to act the same as before, afraid of every new acquaintance I would come across.

It wasn't until three years later that I met a small woman who opened up a huge, colorful world to me. She was not much over five feet tall with a personality five times that size. The moment we first talked, we knew together that life was much more than what we see. At first a romantic relationship formed from this bond. For two years, we shared our hardships. Then we had another two years of complete friendship. I finally knew what life could be like with someone I fully trusted. She was a friend who not only taught me how to open up, but reflected what was good about me. This undersized portion of my own being helped me grow when I all but gave up hope in people. She was a phase in my learning experience that opened the door to "real" life.

Plenty of people come and go in our lives, but few leave a mark in mine. Some have lacerated me deeply and others come with the purpose of mending that wound. I've always felt that if you open yourself to the people around you, they influence your life just by existing around you. I learned this lesson seven years after Nick's accident from a young lady that healed me with her very presence. When she plays a role in my life, all the pain is lifted. She is driven by the need to fix the broken. Her appearance is only that of "white;" not of her skin, not of her hair, not of the clothes she wears. This is just how she appears to me. She has striking beauty with a healing mood. She never has a whole lot to say, but like a whisper, I have to listen closely. This was a time in my life where I had to put my ego aside and let someone try to help. After years of strife and realizing I had many years left, I had to dig out of my darkness. Because of her, I can see the light.

So it's on these rare occasions people can be more than the mindless drones created on "Reality TV." There are people who can help, can heal and can change with you. I have always gotten help when I needed it the most, and it was when I was actually good and ready for them.

The question of having a life after death is something that has always plagued my mind. As a young child, I never even believed there was a Santa Claus, so to try and force me into believing in the church's views never seemed right. I have had particular events happen that have made my opinion sway one way or another, but I realized this age-old question will only be answered upon my own death. Because of a dream I had two months after Nick's death, I have come to the conclusion that there is more. My truth is what I feel inside.

In my dream, I was in a total void. I had other "beings" around me but couldn't make out faces or voices. My guide was a blue-gray figure that I trusted like a part of my own body. He was there just to lead the way and I followed without a second thought. There was a gathering of some sort, but I thought this dark expanse was a weird place for all these "people." Then I noticed Nick and realized this was nothing but a dream. I was again sad, plagued with the same internal struggle. Nick was my older brother and we had fought constantly. Despite our differences, I never doubted the fact that I idolized and loved him. My haunting question was if he had the same feelings for me. Day and night this caused major issues with me. And here he was, in my dream. Suddenly he passed behind me and brushed my left shoulder as he passed. At that instant, there was a blinding light and I awoke. I could feel the touch on my shoulder. It radiated from that point on my body, out, and lifted a weight off my soul. I knew how he felt and it was the same as my feelings for him. He loved me and still wanted to take care of me. As an older brother it was his job! I was transformed. I could smile; a real smile. Not a smile like in my "other" life.

Now fully awake, I went downstairs to eat breakfast. My mom had just returned from a reading with a medium. She was glowing. I thought that she possibly had a "break through" like I just had. She told me what the medium had said and we talked. Little did I know, this would mark a new era in my life. My mom then said, "Oh yeah, the medium also said Nick had a message to pass through to you." She paused, looking slightly confused. "Nick says he feels the same. I don't know what that means, but she said Nick stressed for her to pass this on to you." It made perfect sense to me. Now the dark void of my depression was turning a little less murky.

I fought the "epic battle" for years. Violent storm clouds seemed to follow me every step I took. Depression is easy to spot from an outside perspective, but the internal perspective is sometimes hidden. It was something I just couldn't change. I couldn't fix something I didn't even know was wrong. I saw darkness in every situation. Each right had several wrongs. I was only happy with mild stimulants, had stopped answering phone calls, had stopped talking to friends, had let myself drop out of social functions and slept away the pains of life.

As I look back at my life, portions of my past are blurred or in blackness. I realize that because of some of the traumatic events that have happened I have formed a "safety switch" to turn my consciousness off when needed. I can remember certain things like they just happened moments earlier and other events seem like they never occurred. These are what I call the "voids" in my life.

This went on until one day when I was ready, a friend said, "You're depressed." Simple as that. I saw the light. I saw that I needed to change. Blind as I had become, I was the only one that could change my life. No pills or drink could fix me. It just covered up the problem. Others can help, but the hard work was in my hands. I think of this the way I have heard drug addictions are handled. I will always be able to "slip off the wagon." Depression will never be gone. It will always stick in the back of my head waiting to slowly slip out unnoticed. Listening to the world and to the people around me help me see who I am, because I'm not who I think I am sometimes. I am who the world thinks I am. By my actions, I create myself. I take the smallest leverage I have in life and run with it. There is no use in waiting to change for the better. Everyone deserves warmth and happiness. I have decided there is nothing to do but look for the good. I take it in and really appreciate it. I've realized I am the only one who can make me deeply happy. It is time to stop waiting for life to fall into my hands. I now take life and make it my own!

KEVIN

By Doris Buchanan

I am the mother of a gay son who died of AIDS sixteen years ago. He was 35 years old. I am also the widow of a Presbyterian minister who died of brain tumors thirty-three years ago, just two weeks before I drove Kevin 700 miles to his first year at Vassar College. Kevin was the fourth of five children. These events happened in 1974, long before the word "gay" was synonymous with homosexual, at least for most of us in the mid-west.

My husband, Cal, was diagnosed April 1 of that year with a small spot on his lung. He had surgery to remove the lung which was afflicted, but sixteen days later had many seizures. X-rays found he had multiple inoperable brain tumors. Doctors told us there was nothing they could do for him. When we asked about radiation, they said it might improve him for a period of time but how long they did not know. We took that option and prayed for a miracle. The treatments began early in May and we saw him slowly feeling better. In June he actually felt well enough to attend my graduation from respiratory school and Kevin's from high school. During that well-period in June, he was able to preach one Sunday. We felt so blessed that he was able to participate in these wonderful family events.

Because we were able to find a very fine woman to care for Cal at night, I was able to continue my studies and graduate with my class. I had been working weekends at the hospital since October and agreed to start full time as soon as I graduated. I was able to do so until July 4 when Cal took a sudden turn for the worse. I discussed the situation with my supervisor at the hospital and he agreed to give me a leave of absence for one month. Strangely enough, Cal died one month later on August 5.

A week after the funeral, I returned to work full time. In another two weeks, the time had come to drive Kevin to Vassar College in Poughkeepsie, New York. It was 700 miles from home and my daughter, Laurie, who was a couple years older than Kevin agreed to go with me. That way, I would not be driving home alone, particularly, under the circumstances. Needless to say, I was numb from the trauma of losing my husband, and almost in the same breath losing my son from home. I now had to face fully the responsibility of working full time to pay the bills and continue our family life as much as possible. Neil was the youngest in the family, fifteen years old, still living at home, and going to high school.

Except for the very part-time job I had since October I was, in reality, learning a whole new occupation trying to grasp all the changes now not only in my life but in my children's, keeping my mind on all the new responsibilities at the hospital and praying constantly. I would not only survive for the whole family's sake but truly succeed.

As problems come in bunches, I had one more hurdle before life could return to any semblance of normalcy. During that chaotic summer, I had begun working full time and Neil was having trouble with one infection after another. When I returned home from leaving Kevin at college as a very green freshman, I made an appointment with a specialist for Neil's illness. In the middle of September, he had surgery for his urinary problems. I am happy to report he was a real trooper and everything went according to plan. From then on, we were able to concentrate on our collective and individual grieving.

Going back to Kevin's senior year in high school, he was fully involved in many of the activities of that year and in many ways it was happy and fulfilling for him. I remember how much he enjoyed having a lead roll in the senior play and how I nearly burst with pride to see him on the stage playing his roll so easily and convincingly. I would never have believed that whole year how much he was struggling with something he couldn't tell me or his father, except to say it was painful enough for him to be seeing a school counselor. I had no idea he was struggling with all the fear and confusion of being gay. Whatever it was, I was certainly thankful he was getting counseling. I, of course, did not know who the counselor was. I want to acknowledge him/her for helping Kevin at such a critical time in a way no one else at that point could.

I do know that if he had told me he was gay at that point in time, I would probably have had to ask what that meant. Although I am not able to say just when I became aware of his situation, I am quite sure it dawned on me very slowly. It was probably after he graduated from college and began working at Sotheby's, a prominent art auction house in New York City. I learned much later that by the time Kevin was around 25 years old, all my relatives were aware and I am forever grateful that none of them were ever shocked or had any inclination to reject him. They all really loved him and enjoyed his company. They were all very proud of him for who he was. Homosexuality never seemed to be a factor for my family and relatives as they all liked him too much, as did most people who knew him.

Kevin was always a cheerful little soul, full of fun and laughter with the proverbial sparkle in his eyes. He had many friends all his life. One of my favorite memories was when he was three or four years old. There was a darling little girl the same age that lived next door named Jeanie and they often played together in the neighborhood. One lovely summer day, I was upstairs straightening up the rooms and making the beds when I happened to glance out the window and noticed a front yard down the street about five houses away where a brand new pile of top soil had been dumped apparently earlier that morning. When I looked a little closer, I saw a couple little kids having the time of their lives rolling around and jumping up and down in the blackest of dirt. I watched them for a few moments before going downstairs to phone Jeannie's mother and alert her. I went out the front door to call them home while I walked down the street toward them. They did leave the pile of dirt, but with no great urgency, laughing and giggling all the way home. At least it gave me some time to think about the best way of cleaning Kevin up without getting the black dirt all through the house on his way to the bathtub.

Another story that indicates the kind of person Kevin was came later in life when his partner, Gabriel, was dying of AIDS. After graduating from college, Kevin lived and worked in New York City. He would live there for the rest of his life. He made many friends over the years, but his closest friend eventually became infected with AIDS.

As is the case with most AIDS patients, the disease is fairly slow in developing and the standard medication at that time gave much hope but not much help. Eventually Gabriel's health deteriorated to the point where he had to face the inevitable. He tried to take his own life but without success.

The word spread rapidly, of course, among the group and naturally Kevin hurried over to Gabriel's apartment to see what had happened. I don't know the details, which are not important here, but Kevin was able to persuade him to spend the rest of his days with his family in Miami, Florida with the understanding that he would accompany him home, stay there with him, take care of him and help the family out until the end. Gabriel's mother and siblings knew Kevin and loved him as much as I loved Kevin's friends so they were happy and relieved to have him there. To be able to do this, of course, meant Kevin had to quit his job for those six months. He assured me he had no second thoughts about what he was doing, as he wanted to be with Gabriel as long as possible.

Kevin's death a few years later was comparatively sudden. He hadn't been feeling well for about a year but was still working part time. He had been having trouble with his stomach intermittently and his doctor decided it was time to make an appointment for him to see a specialist immediately after the Thanksgiving holidays. The Sunday before Thanksgiving Day, he became ill and had to stay in bed. By Tuesday morning, one of his friends realized no one had seen or heard from Kevin for a couple days. He held his panic in check, and hurried to Kevin's apartment where he found him in bed. He quickly realized he was delirious. After contacting the doctor, he set things in motion for the ambulance to take him to the hospital where they arrived mid afternoon.

At 6:30 that evening, I received a phone call telling me Kevin was in the hospital and they thought it would be a good idea if I came as soon as possible. They were careful not to alarm me and it wasn't until they called me again at 10:30 that same evening that they had to make it clear I had to come immediately. I called the airlines trying to get a flight out that night but there were no night flights. I told the agent through my tears I had to go to New York because my son was dying. She was struggling to remain professional, but there truly was nothing she could do except put us on a flight the next morning.

Before this turn of events at 10:30, I had been planning on coming the next day with the idea I would be sitting with Kevin through the weekend while he recuperated from this temporary, unnamed illness. I was basing this decision on the fact that Gabriel had been hospitalized more than a couple times, so it seemed reasonable to me that Kevin would have periods of comparative wellness between hospitalizations.

Very sadly, this was not so. My son, Doug, lives not far away. He and I finally left for New York the next morning arriving at Lenox Hospital around noon. My other children, Gail, Laurie and Neil had managed to get there before we did. I don't think any of us were prepared for what awaited us. Kevin had been put on a ventilator the evening before not long after the hospital called me at 6:30. His kidneys had shut down. When we walked into his room, he was barely recognizable with four IV's each dripping a different antibiotic. With all the fluids running into his body and his kidneys no longer functioning every square inch of his body was swollen with those fluids that had no where else to go. I kissed him, sat as close as I could and held his hand, held his hand, and held his hand. Of course I cried, just as I am doing now while writing this.

Sixteen years ago, I knew I could not tell most people how my son had died because of the almost universal prejudice towards homosexuality. I did think it would be just a matter of time before people would see the truth, that homosexuality is not a choice in any sense of the word. I don't know of anyone who chose to be heterosexual. I never did. Did you? If you put your thinking cap on for a moment, who would choose to live a lifestyle where you know instinctively you will be abused verbally, possibly bullied physically, be rejected by many, and even be forsaken by the churches. No matter what some of the clergy try to tell us, I know Christ would not do this.

I will always be very proud of Kevin as I am the rest of my family. All my relatives, even my parents' generation, loved Kevin just the way he was. Kevin was honorable, generous, caring and passionate about his entire life and brought much joy to so many people in so many ways. He demonstrated God's love his whole life, just as Jesus admonishes us to love all peoples.

In 1 Corinthians 13:4-7, we learn that "Love is patient, love is kind. It does not envy, it does not boast, it is not proud. It is not rude, it is not self-seeking, it is not easily angered. It keeps no record of wrongs. Love does not delight in evil, but rejoices with the truth. It always protects, always trusts, always hopes, always perseveres."

Kevin was that kind of person.

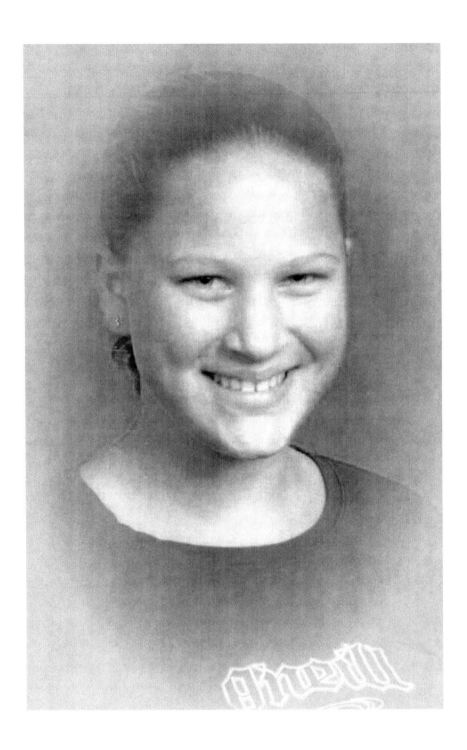

CORRINE'S STORY

A Beautiful Life Cut Short by Bullying

By Rochelle Sides

Corinne Celice Wilson was born on Monday, September 30, 1991 at 2:06 p.m. She was the youngest of four children and the only girl. She was the most beautiful baby with big blue eyes and blonde curly hair. From the day she was born, she was an amazing child. I know that every mother says that, but she was so bright and full of personality. She did everything early. She said her first word at eight months, and walked by eleven months. I should have known then what I was in store for, but as a young mother of four, I just thought it was because she was trying to keep up with her older brothers.

Our family moved to Texas in 1995. Corinne seemed to blossom under all of the love that my husband's family gave her, especially her Grandma Jewel. She fell madly in love with Corinne from the first day, as most people did when they met her. Anyone who spent five minutes with Corinne loved her. She was incredibly beautiful and smart.

That changed when we moved to Rockdale in 2000. Corinne had trouble from the first day she was there. She missed her old school and friends. She didn't feel as if she fit in. I thought that playing a sport would help her to meet people. Unfortunately, joining the team made it worse. In Corinne's first year of playing softball, she was placed on a team with girls who had played together for a considerable amount of time. They teased her relentlessly about her inability to play. She would cry after every practice. They continued to exclude her at practice, which followed through to school.

Corinne would periodically come home from school crying, saying, "No one likes me and I hate it here." I would tell her to try to be nice to one person everyday and soon she would have a friend. It seemed to work, as she did make a friend. The two of them seemed inseparable. Corinne started changing her personality to match that of her new friend. My husband and I thought it was a phase. It came to a head when Corinne and this girl got into trouble at her friend's house. Corrine's father and I ended the relationship, or so we thought. Honestly, prior to that time, Corinne had never misbehaved or gotten into trouble.

For some reason, this girlfriend had a hold on Corinne that we could not break. Corinne did make other friends, but they all included this particular girl. This continued without many problems for the next year and a half. Corinne was now in the sixth grade and really starting to become a beautiful, young girl. Boys were interested in her and vice versa. Corinne was also excelling in academics, as well. I think this is why the bullying began. A group of girls became jealous. At first, they would exclude her, make her cry, and then make up. Then they started to tell Corinne that she was fat and her hair was frizzy. They would make fun of her one day, then befriend her the next. Corinne was so confused. Bullying victims are not always the way they are portrayed in the media. Corinne was almost too beautiful. The bullying was jealousy-based.

In the summer prior to beginning seventh grade, Corinne attended a basketball camp at Baylor University. She had grown a few inches and was starting to be more confident in her appearance and abilities. This made the group's vicious comments and jealousy increase. They started a campaign against Corinne after she had been selected from over 500 contestants to sing in a karaoke contest in Waco. Corinne was so happy and proud of herself.

The jealousy of the group now escalated even more. One day, Corrine came home and said they kept calling her a bragger. They said her hair was frizzy and she couldn't sing. She said she only told them about Waco on one occasion. Their comments must have bothered her. I told her they were not her true friends or they would be proud of her. At the time, I had no idea how bad the bullying had become.

It all came to a head on October 6, 2004. That morning in Phys. Ed. class, one of the girls slapped Corinne and called her a whore. Then that same girl wrote her notes all day, telling her she was fat, ugly, had ratty hair, and that her group of girlfriends all wished she was dead. The note also stated that Corinne should just go home and kill herself. These girls decided that this was the "Theme of the Day". Corinne should go home and kill herself.

I knew my daughter well. She was a very loving and sensitive person. I can only imagine the hurt and confusion she was feeling that day. These girls were supposed to be her best friends and they wanted her dead. That day in one of her classes, Corrine wrote on her desk over and over, "This school hates me." I have been told she had her head down and cried all day. As Corinne left from school that day, these girls said it again, "Just go home and kill yourself!"

School let out early for conferences. Her brothers picked her up as they always did. Corinne asked them to drive by one of the girls so she could talk to her. Her brother told her no, because they needed to get home. Her brother, Richard, left for work at 2:00 p.m. Her brother, Ronald, said she spent the entire afternoon drawing horns on girls' pictures, running up and down the stairs, and running in and out of my bedroom. Later, we found out she had been trying to find a gun. Ronald left for work just before 4:00 p.m. and I was home by 4:45 p.m. I found her dead from a single gunshot wound to her forehead.

Corinne left no note, which makes me believe she did not want to die. She just wanted a break from the pressure. She needed to show these girls how bad they were hurting her. She was looking forward to performing in the rodeo so very much. We know she would never want her father and me to be upset so we believe Corinne really thought she would just get hurt, spend some time in the hospital, and everything would be fixed. Of course, this did not happen. Instead of listening to our daughter perform at the rodeo, her father and I buried her.

The pain of losing Corrine is immeasurable. My husband wrote in her eulogy that they say you don't know what you have until it is gone. But we knew. We knew Corinne was an amazingly beautiful, talented, and loving person. She made everyday spent with her a better day. We lost everything on October 6, 2004, and the world lost more than it will ever know.

The school administration denied knowing something was going on that day. I let them know that was hard to believe. We had students come to us at Corrine's visitation and tell us what had gone on with the girls and Corinne. I asked the principal, "Didn't they come to you?" His reply was, "No." I told the principal that he should question why the students didn't feel comfortable reporting this type of behavior to him. Also at the visitation, I had three parents come to me with their children's stories. While the principal and administration denied that the school has a problem with bullying, I was told by parents that one child was on a suicide watch, one child had talked about suicide, and one child had been in counseling for bullying-related issues for an entire year.

Corinne was not the only child who committed suicide in Rockdale. Two years earlier, a transgender boy, who was incessantly bullied by a group of classmates, took his own life. On the day of his suicide, he had been followed home by a group of boys. He was urinated upon and thrown into a garbage dumpster. When a witness came forward with the facts, the police said there was no proof. This is just another case of society failing to seek justice for innocent victims.

With Corrine's suicide, there were no repercussions and no consequences for the girls. To this day, the school does not have an anti-bullying policy or anti-bullying program in place. Internally, I cannot make sense of Corinne's suicide. What I have to do is make something come out of it. I don't know what would happen to me if I didn't do this. How else do you survive?

Shortly after Corinne's death, I went to my computer and typed in "anti-bullying". Brenda High's www.bullypolice.org site came up. I filled out the parent survey and Brenda called me. I trusted her because she knows what it is like to lose a child to bullying-related suicide. Jared and Corinne were exactly the same age when they took their own lives, thirteen years, six days. She told me the Bully Police USA organization was healing for her. She assured me that watching a governor sign anti-bully legislation is healing.

Prior to joining www.bullypolice.org, I didn't want to get out of bed. I didn't want to work. If Corinne's tragedy could help save one child, I knew I was doing the right thing.

Jamie, another girl who had been rejected by Corinne's tormentors, gave me solace. She told me that on October 6, when the bullies were telling Corinne to kill herself, Corinne's reply was, "Don't worry, God has a plan for me." I will go forward and do all I can to be sure that Corinne did not die in vain. I know today that Corinne saved Jamie's life. Jamie's mother let me know that Corinne, in befriending Jamie, saved Jamie from suicide.

Corinne is a beautiful person.

Corrine's mother, Rochelle Sides, is now serving as the Co-Director of *Bully USA Police* and Director of *Bully Police Texas*, a watch-dog group that advocates for children who are bullied and help enact anti-bullying laws.

www.CorinneWilson.com
www.bullypolice.org
jrsides (at) classicnet (dot) net

ALWAYS IN ALL WAYS

In Memory of Megan My Tormoehlen

By Deb Tormoehlen

Megan My Tormoehlen was my first born, a beautiful daughter. After her birth, the nurse brought her to me and took her little fingers to touch my cheek. Through my entire pregnancy, I dreamed of a beautiful baby girl. She was so petite that I carried her even when she was a toddler. My mother would say, "Put her down and let her walk!" I needed her to be close to me. We had a special connection. We were attached at the hip and heart. When I nursed her, I would marvel at how beautiful she was and how good it felt cradling her in my arms.

Megan was my mentor long before either one of us realized it. I entered nursing school, a divorced mother of three. Megan was five, Melissa was three and Michael was one. When I first started school, Megan My would barricade the front door with her arms outstretched attempting to stop me from leaving. I had to pick her up and hand her to my mother or sister, Deanna, so I could attend class. After awhile, she was my biggest supporter saying, "Go to school and get an A star 100." Upon my graduation, she proudly displayed my diploma to the audience.

I met her adoptive father shortly after graduation. We married three years later. Megan couldn't wait to call him "Daddy." Within four years, she had two more brothers Matthew and Marcus, whom she loved so. She carried them around like little rag dolls. Megan played a little soccer but softball and basketball were her favorites. What she didn't possess in athletic skill she possessed in heart. She always had a smile on her face and oh what a beautiful smile it was. Her giggle was infectious.

During her teens, she wrote a beautiful poem to me, entitled "Mom", which is framed and sits on my dresser. The last two sentences said, "Someday I hope I can be as good a mother to my children as you have been to me. You're not only my mother, but my best friend." Megan never became a mother, and I never became a grandmother to her children. We were both cheated of this joy.

On January 26, 1992, Super Bowl Sunday, we were together at a family party. She left shortly before halftime. She kissed everyone goodbye. I received the last kiss. She touched my cheeks with her fingers, just as she had done at her birth, and kissed me goodbye. I told her I loved her and to wear her seatbelt.

At 8:06 p.m., Megan's car was hit by a train as she was driving home. The railroad crossing had no lights or gates. Her view had been obstructed by trees and shrubs, the road was on an incline, and the crossing was at an angle. It was a horrible, unsafe railroad crossing. It was a death trap.

In March, 1992, I began circulating petitions in Ohio and Michigan for lights and gates at all railroad crossings. I took petitions to neighbors, to work, to Bedford High School, to my husband's work, to family and to friends. I obtained an attorney, attempting to begin a lawsuit against the Michigan Department of Transportation (MDOT) and the railroad company. I discovered the only way to obtain information regarding the railroad company was to sue.

While looking through records, it became apparent that a supervisor for MDOT neglected requests for an investigation of that crossing on at least three different occasions and never authorized a formal investigation. All he needed to do was sign his name. His signature was mandatory for an investigation to proceed. He had done nothing! It took the death of a 19 year-old woman for the supervisor to do what he should have done years before.

I wrote letters to the editors of local newspapers in Monroe, Michigan and in Toledo, Ohio regarding the negligence of this supervisor and the railroad company. In my letters, I questioned why this man and this department were not accountable for their lack of action. Our government has checks and balances. Why not the MDOT? During the lawsuit, footnotes requesting an investigation went unheeded. Mysteriously, the footnotes disappeared when we rechecked records. My lawyer asked where the footnotes had gone, but they denied removing them. When shown the copies, MDOT representatives replied, "We can't be sued because we are MDOT!" Apparently the public cannot sue the State of Michigan. Ultimately, I was told I could not sue MDOT and this supervisor.

Why was this supervisor not held accountable for not doing his job? I feel he will eventually be held accountable by God. I often wonder how he looks himself in the mirror each day, especially if he has children. Money and power makes some people above the law. My only comfort is that I do believe in karma.

I spoke in Lansing, Michigan before MDOT, congressmen, senators, the railroad company and their high-priced attorneys. The railroad company was requesting passage of a bill that would exempt them from lawsuits for negligence by public citizens like me. I spoke on what would have been Megan's twentieth birthday, November 13, 1992. This was the first birthday after her passing. I begged them not to allow such a law to pass. The bill was defeated, maybe in part because of my tearful pleas. I know my daughter gave me the strength and encouragement to speak before this group. Afterwards, I broke down sobbing. The loss of a child is the most agonizing, unnatural event in the circle of life. Children bury their parents and bring them flowers, not the other way around.

Finally in January, 1995, lights and gates were erected at the horrible railroad crossing where my daughter lost her life and our family was forever changed and saddened. The investigation did, in fact, prove that crossing to be a "critical crossing" which by definition "needs lights and gates." These should have been up years ago. My petitions had been instrumental in making this happen, and made this crossing safer three years after Megan's passing. They came too late to save my daughter or spare us the anguish of losing her, but hopefully, she and I spared another family our heartache and sorrow.

Our family was forever changed by the loss of our daughter, sister, granddaughter, niece, cousin. Our second daughter, Melissa, misses her big sister, Megan, and lives without the special ties that bond sisters. Shortly after losing Megan, our oldest son said, "Mom, you used to smile all the time. Now it seems like you never smile." Our youngest boys, Matthew and Marcus, barely remember their big sister except through stories remembered, tears, and laughter. They know the "Mom-Who-Lost-Megan My". They don't know the mom before that loss. My husband, Doug, and I struggled to stay together. Everyone in our family has struggled. We were all cheated of having Megan in our lives.

Our daughter, Megan My, was a gift from God, and I consider it the greatest honor to be chosen as her mother. I would not trade the gift of having her and losing her, for never having known her. I am a better person from having her in my life. Now that I'm further down the road, I do smile more easily. To this day my daughter teaches me life's lessons of courage, kindness, patience, hope, and the greatest of all, love. She lives on within all of her family, making us better from her presence in our lives. I must do her short, sweet life justice. I hear her angelic voice whispering to me, "My happiness is intertwined with yours. I want happiness and fond memories for all of you, for I live on within all of you and you live deep within my heart." I owe this to her and to all who love her.

I hope I have made you proud, my Megan My.

You are my love always, in all ways.

Mom

BLESSINGS

In Loving Memory of
William Jerome Hertzfeld Jr. (Billy)
February 18, 1980 – January 1, 1999

By Leslie Kay Hertzfeld

Full of life, love and laughter,
He touched many hearts and spoke to our souls
With his caring and comical ways.

It was a wonderful Christmas. Everyone was home. I look at my life and realize how great it is. December 17, 1998, our fifth grandchild was born. She was such a blessing. I can't think of anything better than a new baby for Christmas. Faith was so tiny when she came into this world. Her cousins couldn't get enough of her. Morgan, Drake, Dane, and Nathan were all so eager to take their turns holding her.

I have a wonderful family. My husband and I have five daughters and one son. We live on the farm where all of our children grew up. I have such wonderful memories of them playing together. We are looking forward to New Year's Eve. Our whole family gets together and we go bowling and eat afterwards. The adults and the kids all have a great time. It is such a blessing that we are all together.

I spend my days enjoying my grandchildren and painting. Being an artist is very special to me. I paint portraits, pets, and landscapes. Painting is what I am supposed to do. It brings me such joy. I feel like the angels are helping me. Yes, life is good. I never worried about life being too good. I never knew that it could change in an instant. But it did.

Our Father who art in heaven, hallowed be thy name . . . (breathe . . . breathe . . . just breathe) Thy kingdom come, Thy will be done on earth as it is in heaven (breathe . . . breathe . . . God help me) Give us this day our daily bread and forgive us our trespasses as we forgive those who trespass against us . . . (breathe, I can't remember to breathe . . .) and lead us not into temptation but deliver us from evil for Thine is the kingdom, and the power and the glory forever and ever. Amen.

Oh . . . Billy . . . Billy . . . Billy, oh how I miss you. Dear God, please take care of my Billy. Our Father who art in heaven . . . (breathe . . . just breathe) and so it goes on, hour after hour. I seem to be in a fog. As I come back to the reality of what has just happened, I find myself with my forehead leaning on the icy cold window pane saying the Lord's Prayer over and over. I keep telling myself to remember to breathe. Why can't I remember to breathe? My only son has gone home to be with the Lord. I know there should be some comfort in that but I find myself wondering where his angels were. You hear all of the stories about how angels came and helped someone survive. Where were Billy's angels? Did they come to warn me and I didn't hear them? Could I have saved him? Oh my

God, help me. (breathe, Leslie, just breathe . . .) I pray for the strength to get through this, I pray for my husband who has lost his only son, I pray for my daughters who have lost their baby brother, and I pray for Billy that God will take care of him. (breathe . . . breathe . . .)

That New Years Eve in 1998 was the day our lives changed forever. On one hand, it seems so long ago and on the other it is like yesterday. One moment you have a wonderful life, and the next a part of you is missing. It takes a lot of energy to pretend that everything is okay. You try to carry on a reasonably intelligent conversation while part of you is still screaming on the inside that your son is gone. Someone please say his name. Tell me you remember him. But very few have the courage to say what you are dying to hear. They say, "How are you," and you reply, "I'm okay." You realize that you too have lost the ability to say what you want to. So these meaningless little conversations take place. As you walk on you think, "Oh, I wanted to let her know how much I miss my son, how hard it is to get up in the morning, how hard it is to go into the grocery store and see his favorite foods, watch TV and see shows he liked and yet I say I'm okay." We talk uncomfortably and she walks on thinking, "I wish I would have said something. I didn't want to make her cry, she looks so sad. Will it ever get better for her?" The answer for me is, "No, it never got better."

I am thankful that for some it does. I just learned how to deal with it a little better. I know now that words aren't always necessary. Sometimes it's a silent hug, those few moments when souls come together, those few moments of utter understanding that there really are no words, only love and compassion. This year marks the end of the tenth year without Billy here with us. He wasn't sick. Actually he was a tall, very good looking young man. He was so funny and so very kind, always looking out for the underdog.

I remember a young man at the funeral who stood there for the longest time. I asked him if he was alright because he seemed so moved by what had happened to Billy. He told me that he was at a basketball game and he had forgotten his shoes so he couldn't play. Billy had just gotten a new pair of those shoes all of us mothers stood in line for. You know the ones that were so expensive back in the day. Well, Billy just took off those shoes and sat there in his stocking feet so this young man could play. Billy had never told me about that. I was always grateful that this young man who said he didn't really know Billy that well took the time to come say goodbye. It was just one of the many blessings that we would learn to see and cherish forever.

But wait, I don't want to get ahead of myself. It is hard to make myself think back and remember what happened to Billy. I have spent so much energy trying not to remember it. I know that I will never forget it. I just try to keep it in the back of my mind.

It was New Years Eve, 1998. After much pleading, I agreed to take my son to a party just a few country roads away. I didn't want him to go. I actually pleaded with him. It was almost 10:30 p.m. "Why go so late?" "Oh Mom," he said. "I really don't want to go either, but since I've been working nights I haven't seen anyone since graduation." Billy was a drummer and had just gotten his set of DW drums and a truck that he loved. He was so responsible I said okay and I DROVE HIM. I still have a hard time with that. When he didn't come home, we started to check and that's when our lives changed. The police came, our friends came, and the search began. I prayed that he would be okay. Would we ever see him again? But as the day drew on, we knew this was real. Billy was missing. (Oh my God . . . I can't breathe . . .)

It was bitter cold that night. A storm was forming. We had to find him. I stayed at home with the grandchildren, while everyone searched. I tried to be calm, kept the coffee going, tried not to scare the grandkids. Friends and family drove trucks, rode on snowmobiles and some even walked. Cold, cold, cold. I can't stand the cold to this day. Then it happened. Someone came to the door and said they found him. I went, but I can't remember who with. Someone stayed with the grandchildren, I don't know who. I just remember all of the flashing lights and all of the sad faces as I got out of the car . . . or was it a truck . . . and there was Bill, my husband. "He's gone, he's gone." We held each other and I could hear myself saying, "No, no, no!"

My Billy was frozen into the ground under the road in a cement culvert. He had no coat on. He was so cold. Our daughter, Amy, crawled down into the ditch. Yes, she knew it was her baby brother. That sight is still with her. There is so much to this story. Why didn't Billy have the brand new coat on that he bought with his own money? He never would have left it behind. Who put him in that culvert, and why? How could they just leave him there? Why weren't his "friends" talking? What happened to our son? So many questions I would love to have answered. To this day, we never found out what actually happened at that party. I often hoped that someone would investigate again, or that someone who was at the party would come forward so we could finally stop wondering. It took a long time, but I now pray for those who have to carry the heavy burden of what happened to our Billy.

This is not a story of guilt and who did what to whom, but a story of blessings that are always there if we will just see them. God has a plan. He carries us when we can't go on. He sends help in books, music and bumper stickers. We just have to look.

Now as I look back, our blessings started when WE FOUND HIM. So many people are still searching for their loved ones, still seeing them in crowds only for it to not be them. They are still waiting for the phone to ring. We had found our son.

I wish I could have saved him. I wish I hadn't taken him to his friend's house. I wish he was still playing his drums, still laughing, still playing with the grandkids. He had so much potential. Billy would have been a great dad, a wonderful husband, and he always would have been a very special brother to his five older sisters. He was a brother they could count on. I need to look back, remember to breathe, see the blessings God has given us. They are the reason I know Billy is alive in heaven.

There was a white dove that sat on Billy's truck after his passing. It was all alone, in the cold and snow. We just kept watching that dove. It stayed right on Billy's truck. It was just sitting there looking in the kitchen window watching us, like he was on guard. When we walked into the church hall for the lunch after the funeral, we saw that the hall ceiling was covered with white doves hanging from strings made from white paper doilies. I wondered who knew about our special dove. Who had made all of these doves? How wonderful it was to have all those doves watching over Billy's funeral. We found out later that they had been left from a children's event. Another blessing because I felt they were from Billy and he was saying, "See, I am okay. I am with you always."

The morning of the funeral, the prosecuting attorney called and said they had decided to do an autopsy and they would pick Billy up after the funeral. I couldn't believe what I was hearing. I didn't even know you could have a funeral and not go to the cemetery. What a blow! As we were going over to the church hall after the funeral, I realized that this was also a blessing. There was such a bad storm after Billy passed. It was a miracle that anyone was able to get to the funeral. We were able to have everyone who came go right into the hall and not fight the bitter cold to get to the cemetery. This was especially good for the older people who came. They picked Billy up and did the autopsy. We waited for them to give our son back to us. We then had a private service before we went to the cemetery. The first time was hard, but the second time was something that words cannot express.

My whole life changed after Billy passed. Yes, I knew he was in a better place, but I wasn't ready to let him go. He was only eighteen years old, so full of life, so young! I thought he needed to graduate from college, he needed to fall in love and get married, and, yes, I needed to hold his children in my arms and love them as I loved their father.

I began to realize that the little things that were happening were messages from the other side. They were signs that if I took the time to recognize them, they would be the blessings that would help me through this.

During the days following Billy's passing, I never went anywhere alone. I couldn't drive. I couldn't pay at the register without breaking down. Still today, I can't walk through the grocery store without seeing Billy's favorite foods. Then I just stand there. People must think I'm nuts, but I am just reliving a cherished memory. I now look at people differently as I walk past them in the store. I try to smile at those who look like they need a smile. I am patient when the person in front of me seems confused and can't find something. I remember how it was to be there, to use all of your energy just to get through the day and still fight to remember to breathe.

I am starting to see more blessings. I am still not sleeping well, still struggling to breathe, still trying to be what everyone wants me to be.

One day, I went with my husband to the store. For no reason, I started to cry. I couldn't stop. I faced the shelves while Bill rushed on to get what we needed. I sat down on a box so embarrassed that I couldn't stop crying. "Oh God," I prayed, "Please help me." (breathe . . . breathe . . . breathe . . .) Suddenly a feeling of peace came over me. I felt warm and strangely okay. I sat there breathing calmly, with a feeling of warmth all around me. Then my phone rang. It was my daughter, Amy. "Mom, are you okay?" She said her sons, Drake, age five, and Dane, age three, were bouncing on the bed and she didn't have the heart to stop them because they said they were playing with Billy. They just came out and said Billy couldn't play anymore because something is wrong with Grandma and he had to go help her. I could feel his arms around me bringing peace and love. Yes, yes, another blessing. Billy is alive and well on the other side and able to see and hear us.

One day, I was talking to Billy as I usually did when in the car. I looked up and told him, "I can't believe I don't see you in the clouds since I am always looking up now." When I got home, I told Bill to take time to look up because the clouds were so beautiful. A few days later, Bill called and said, "Go out on the porch and look up at the clouds. They are beautiful!" I said, "Okay." I was doing the dishes. I was too tired to go. I'll just tell him I looked. No, Bill took the time to call, I must go. When I looked up in the sky, there was a huge cloud of a person waving. His arm was raised high above his head, his other hand was on his hip, the blue sky shone between his legs. I thank God my daughter, Angela, was there to get the camera because I couldn't move. Billy had answered my prayer and I have a picture to prove it. When Bill got home, I thanked him for telling me about the cloud. He said he didn't see that cloud, he was telling me about the one on the other side of the house. I know God had a hand in my seeing Billy's cloud. The back porch is right off the kitchen where I was doing dishes, and the front porch is on the other side of the house. For some reason, I went to the front porch. Another blessing.

I believe my turning point was when I painted a portrait of Billy. It had been six long months since his passing with long sleepless nights, even longer days. One Sunday morning, I woke up with the knowledge that today I was to paint Billy. No, no I couldn't. I was too tired. The voice in my right ear was persistent. I had to do it. The energy in the room was so strong it made the hairs on the back of my neck stand up. Oh yes, I could do it. Billy fairly flew onto the paper. The energy never left, it always talking . . . "Do this, no do that, gently, gently, yes, yes, that's it." Then it was done. I was exhausted. It was Billy with all his sparkle. But wait. As I turned from the table, I looked back over my shoulder. Oh, I need to pink up his cheeks. The energy was no longer with me but it didn't matter. I wanted to pink his cheeks, so I did. There, it was done. I look at this painting and it is like he is truly with me. I am so thankful for this painting of my son. I am so thankful for the angels that helped me to paint it, because it is a gift from heaven above.

Sometime later, I went to a psychic still looking for answers as to what happened to my son. She said, "Oh, you painted a picture of your son. Well, he wants you to know that he doesn't like the pink spots on his cheeks. He was with you when you painted it, but you couldn't hear him try to stop you." Yes, another blessing. I thought the painting was a blessing, but Billy was there too. I left the pink as a reminder of his presence.

I lay awake at night thinking of Billy. Can he see me? Does he know how much I miss him? I know that his loss will always be with me. I will never be able to make it go away. I heard once that I would grieve two to three minutes at a time for the rest of my life. I know that it is okay to grieve and it is also okay not to grieve. It is okay to be in the moment with your family and friends. It is okay to be happy, even if it's only for a moment. I had a difficult time thinking at the beginning of this journey. I just tried to breathe. I tried to hang on to the thought that I was okay. I hung on for the few moments when I would feel okay and then I would slip back into the grief that surrounded me. Now, I have come full circle. I have more good days than bad. Now, I am able to embrace the grief when it comes. I know that it lasts a few moments and then I will feel my angels around me and I will have peace again.

Over the years, I have grown so much. I have learned to watch for the blessings. I have learned to forgive those who hurt us. I have learned that no matter what happens, it isn't as bad as losing Billy. I would like to share one of Billy's messages with you. He said, "Dying is like taking off an old coat and stepping into glory. If you could see what I see, you would never wish me back." Most of all, I have learned that Billy's angels were with him when he passed. He did not go alone. They carried him in their loving arms up to heaven for they were sent from God Himself to bring Billy home.

I have my family and I am so thankful for them. Since Billy passed, Angela has blessed us with two more grandchildren, Phoenix and Destiny, and the new baby is due in June. Then there are the blessings, sent from heaven above, that keep me going.

Before Billy passed, I loved to paint. I enjoyed putting people's thoughts and memories on paper. I knew they would always enjoy them. Now, after losing Billy and after painting his picture, I know that this work is gifted. I always prayed before beginning a painting, but now I realize just how powerful this blessing is. I feel so blessed to have the opportunity to create this art. I look at Billy's picture and I know it was gifted to me, not by me. I knew then that I wanted to help others who have lost a loved one.

I have always known there was something I was meant to do with this gift God has given me. I could feel the calling. Deep inside, there was more. I would help others with my art, but I didn't know how. Every time I looked at Billy's picture, I knew there was more for me to do, but what?

One day, my daughter, Angela, had an idea for an angel magnet that would honor our loved ones and I was blessed when she asked me to be a part of it. Angela wanted me to draw and paint the angel that would be perfect for our magnet. I prayed about the angel magnet and asked for guidance. I knew that this angel magnet would help those of us who are walking this path of sadness. I knew it should be an angel holding our loved one's name in their arms. I believe the angel magnet was sent to help us get through this most difficult time in our lives.

The angel refrigerator magnet is there first thing in the morning to help us start another day. It's there in the middle of the night when we can't sleep. It's there so we can have a moment of peace, a moment to feel the loving energy of our loved one around us. It's there for us to take a moment to remember something funny or just to say their name so we can hear the sound of it. Many times we get so stuck on the loss that we can't think of anything else. But for that moment in time, when we gaze at the name our angel is holding, we can remember something about them other than the loss. We can be free of the pain even it's for only a second because maybe tomorrow it will be for two seconds. Then one day, we will be able to let go of the "whys" of it and be able to feel the love again. We will have taken a small step each morning by remembering some happy memory about our loved one.

I have an angel magnet on the back of my car. I believe that people are afraid to mention our loved ones because they don't want to hurt us. I believe that my magnet lets people know that it's okay to say Billy's name. I want to talk about him. I come out of the store and see my magnet and feel better. I can't explain why, I just do.

My daughter, Angela, and I have started a business called *Inspired To Be*. We believe that your loved ones deserve to be honored for how they touched your lives, and we understand that you need to cherish them because of the love you shared and the love they are still sending you. We know that you still think of them, you still love them, and you still remember them. Our purpose is to create unique and inspirational gifts for your loved ones. Angela writes the poetry and I paint the pictures. Our company will help you to honor those who have already passed and to celebrate those still here. We also want you to be able to express your love, appreciation, thanks, and sympathy to the people in your life with a gift that is meaningful, personal, and has an inspirational message. We are always working on creating new gifts for you to share with your family and friends.

Inspired To Be created the *Because of Billy Fund* in loving memory of William Jerome Hertzfeld Jr., "Billy", full of life, love, and laughter. He touched many hearts and spoke to our souls with his caring and comical ways. He was always there to lend a helping hand to anyone in need. So in his honor, we would like to reach out our hearts and hands to those in need and give **Because of Billy**. You can read more about Billy on our "About Us" page.

All of the blessings I have received are the reason that I know my Billy is okay in heaven. I will see him again someday. The most precious blessing that I have been given has been a chance to help those who also walk this path. Every time I have done a painting of a loved one, every time I have talked to someone and heard their story, and every time I have mailed an angel magnet, I have healed a little more. I pray that they have also been able to heal because they have talked and shared their story. I pray that each time they tell their story, it gets a little easier.

I would like to thank you for allowing me to be a part of this very difficult journey. May God bless you on your journey and remember to look for the blessings.

Love and blessings, Leslie Kay Hertzfeld

Our angel magnet was the inspiration behind Angela and I creating our company, *Inspired To Be*. We love to be able to create gifts that bring comfort and peace to those with a grieving heart.

www.inspiredtobe.com
In Loving Memory of William Jerome Hertzfeld Jr.

Dearly missed by:
Mom—Leslie, Dad—Bill
Sisters—Julie, Amy, Jenny, Angela, and Becky
Brother-In-Laws—Scott, Cory, Michael, and Rod
Nieces—Morgan, Faith, Destiny, and Adelyn
Nephews—Drake, Dane, Nathan, and Phoenix

Together in Heaven with:
Grandpa Lester and Grandma Ruthie
Grandpa Clarence and Grandma Alice

IN THE MIDST OF LIFE

By Angela Hall

"In the midst of life, we wonder why,
we stop, we stare, we start to cry.
We wonder why it has to end,
or is it here, we begin again." ©

Time is a funny thing. It flies by so fast and yet it can also be very slow at the same time. Have you ever noticed how a smell, a song, or something someone says can take you back in time? You go back to memories that can never be replaced, a time when all was well. I often go back to the summer of 1994. I was nineteen, newly engaged, and planning my wedding for October 14, 1995. I had no worries, just which wedding dress I was going to pick for the big day. Life was wonderful. I was going to school to be an accountant, a CPA. I wanted to own my own business and be a success. I had everything planned. Silly me.

It was October 6, 1994 and I got up as usual in the morning to get ready for work. The weird thing about that morning was that I kept giggling, like I was being watched. I didn't think anything of it and off to work I went. The day seemed pretty normal. It was almost time for my morning break. I always took my break at 10:30 a.m. and suddenly at 10:17 a.m. something was telling me to call my fiancé's mother right away. I left for break early and went to my car to call his mother. When she answered, the phone, I knew that something wasn't right. She said, "Angie, you need to get here as soon as you can and be careful." I said, "What is wrong? Is he o.k.?" She replied, "Just be careful." I knew something was really wrong. My heart started pounding and I started to cry. I ran back into work to tell my boss that I had to leave, that something was wrong with my fiancé. My boss knew that I was in no condition to drive and had a co-worker drive me to my future mother-in-law's house.

A usually short trip was now an eternity. There was a part of me that didn't want the trip to end because then I wouldn't be faced with reality. If I were in the car, then everything was as I always knew it to be; wonderful. I kept thinking, how bad is it? Is he okay? What happened? But, I knew deep in my heart, the truth. When I arrived at his mother's house, I saw his uncle and grandmother pulling out of the driveway. His grandmother saw me and her jaw went slack. She placed her hand over her mouth to cover her gasp. Now I knew something was really wrong. The reality of all of this was so close. I didn't want to know, but I had to find out. I could no longer stall time. I got out of the car, and my mom and dad came running out of the house. My dad grabbed me and hugged me. He said, "He's gone, Angie. He's gone." I was so confused that I couldn't grasp what he was telling me. Suddenly I realized and I fell to the ground with great sobs. I kept thinking in my mind, "But he was just here! Everything was wonderful. He was just here."

After finding out that he had fallen asleep at the wheel on his way to work that morning, I was in shock. I remembered the feeling I had that morning of being watched. I realized he would have already been gone while I was readying for work. I started remembering more things as time went on. About two weeks before his passing, a friend of ours died in a car accident on his way to work. He also fell asleep while driving. My fiancé kept saying, "But I just saw him at the gas station. I can't believe he's gone." Immediately I was heartbroken for his girlfriend and I said aloud, "I could never go through that. She must be devastated." I had no idea that fate would soon have me living that same reality.

I also realized how much we talked about death and what happens when one passes on. My fiancé always said how he would look after me. I didn't know what I was being prepared for. I thought we were just talking. He always wanted to make sure I knew how much he loved me. He would say, "If I were to die tomorrow, would you know how much I love you?" Each time I would say, "Yes." I thought he was just a romantic. A few days before his passing, he wanted to make sure I knew how much he loved me, but his tone was different this time. He really needed to make sure that I knew what I meant to him. I reassured him that I knew what he felt for me. He also wanted me to tell my family how much he loved all of them. I thought he was being silly, but he was very serious that I tell everyone how he felt. I said that I would. I did not know he was getting ready to say goodbye. I wish I would have known what was going to happen, but I couldn't. Now I can see clearly what everything was leading up to, but I didn't see then. I didn't know.

On the morning of his passing, I woke him up for work. I remember seeing him lying there, looking so peaceful. He got up and got ready for work. Before he left, he knelt down and hugged me and sobbed. I asked him what was wrong and he told me again how much he loved me and that he didn't want to leave. I told him that everything would be okay, and that I would see him that night after work. But, he continued sobbing. When he finally did leave, he stood in the doorway and turned to look at me without saying a word. Something felt different about the way he looked into my eyes. It was like he looked deep within my heart and soul. After he walked out, I prayed for him. I prayed to God and his angels to protect him and take care of him. After doing so for about fifteen minutes, a peace came over me and I fell back to sleep. I found out that he passed approximately fifteen minutes after he left my house.

As time went on and I remembered certain things he had said to me, I wondered if a part of him knew what was about to happen. He always would ask me what I was going to do when I wasn't going to be an accountant. I said, "I don't know what you are talking about. Of course I will be an accountant." He would smile and say, "No you won't, you will change your mind." I would get frustrated because I couldn't understand why I would go in a different direction. I had a plan.

Well, he was right. After his passing, I began writing poetry. This was a way for me to get out what I was feeling about losing him. I was writing all about my heartbreak, my sorrow, and if I could change anything, I would. It was a healing process for me and I always felt better when I was writing. So, I decided to take a poetry class at a local college and see what I could learn. My teacher gave us an assignment to write about a tragedy, but we couldn't let the reader know until the very end of the poem that it was a tragedy. I knew what I would be writing about. It was hard, but I knew that each time I wrote about it, I healed a little bit more.

This is the poem that I wrote for my poetry class:

Memories

Catching my eye from the corner,
where he casually stood.
I stared for seconds at a time,
for he was looking good.

He waltzed on up to my table,
asking me for a dance.
Looking in his eyes I said,
"Thank you for the chance."

We were by each other's side,
since the day we met,
I was hoping someday soon,
a wedding date we'd set.

With a shy smile and ring in hand,
asking me for his wife.
A tiny tear fell on my face,
as I accepted for life.

The big event was a year away,
and the plans were being made.
He was carefully choosing his groomsmen,
and the dresses were the color of jade.

His mother phoned me on Thursday,
wanting to talk to me.
The news she told was unbelievable,
I said, "It cannot be."

The room was full of family and friends,
the scent of flowers in the air.
He was lying peacefully in the casket,
with my fingers through his hair. ©

Everything changed for me when I began writing. I knew in my heart that this was a path I was meant to walk. A little over four years after losing my fiancé, tragedy struck again. My only brother, my baby brother, Billy, passed away on New Year's Eve, 1998. He was only eighteen years old. Life as I knew it changed again. Why was this happening? I remember thinking to myself, I can't do it again. I can't do it. I don't want to do it. I don't want the sleepless nights, the crying until I can't cry another tear; the heartache, the questions, the confusion, the sorrow, the trying to get back on your feet, and the figuring out how to live without them. I did not want to keep going, but I knew I had to. I had to do it for my parents, my family, myself. I had no choice but to keep going forward. I owed it to my fiancé and my brother to keep going on my journey. I knew I couldn't go back in time and have them in my life again. I had to move forward and see where their loss would take me. Deep down I felt that I wanted to use what I might learn through my own grief and loss to help others in similar situations.

After Billy's passing, I couldn't sleep at all. I was going on day three with very little sleep. I finally fell into a deep sleep. When I awoke, I had an urgency to write a poem. I fought it as long as I could because I was so tired. But, I struggled out of bed and grabbed my pen and paper. The words practically flew onto the paper. I knew it wasn't me who was writing this poem. This was coming from the heavens. I knew it was Billy's message to our family and friends. This poem was such a blessing. After I wrote it down, I read it to my parents. They wanted it to be read at his funeral. The response that people had about the poem was unbelievable. People told me how deeply it touched them and some said that it helped them through their own loss. I knew then that I needed to write, not just for myself, but for others. We need messages from our loved ones, and they want to send them to us.

I was so touched by everyone's reaction that I knew I needed to do more, but what? People began asking me to write poems for them from their loved ones. I was also getting requests for weddings, new babies, anniversaries, birthdays and baptisms. It was hard to believe that people would want me to write for them. I knew when I would write for someone, something would happen. I felt I was being guided by the angels. I knew then that I was not meant to be an accountant. All of my loss, pain, sorrow and grief had led me to this point. I found that through the gift of writing, I was able to help others through their losses with a positive, inspirational message that they could hear over and over. Even though I was carrying the loss of my own loved ones, it was very healing for me to be there for others in their time of need. I was told that whenever they were having a hard time, they read their poem, and felt more at peace. I found comfort in knowing that I could help in some way. But as time went on, I kept feeling that I still wasn't doing enough to help others. There was more that had to be done.

During the five years after my brother's passing, I met a wonderful man, got married and had a son named Phoenix. Blessings were coming my way and I was embracing them with open arms. Right before my son's first birthday, my husband got the call. His mother was diagnosed with stage four lung cancer and had three months to a year to live. We couldn't believe this was happening. She was so young, so full of life. She was only going in for some testing because she wasn't feeling well. I didn't know what to do or say to my husband. This was his mom. They were so close. He adored her. My son hadn't even really gotten to know her yet. I was at a loss for words. How can I help my family? I knew the road we were headed down and it was not going to be easy.

As we tried to let the news sink in, my grandpa was put into the hospital right across the hall from my mother-in-law. He was also dying from cancer. He had been ill for quite some time. A couple of months before my mother-in-law was diagnosed, she would talk to me about what my mom must have been going through with the impending loss of her father. I couldn't believe in such a short period of time that she was across the hall from him also dying of cancer. I was stunned.

A few days after we heard the news about the amount of time she had left, my husband received another call. They were now telling him that she only had three to five days to live. We were shocked, heartbroken, devastated and we were dreading what lay ahead. On our way to the hospital, I kept thinking something had to be done for our loved ones; those that were passing on, and those who would be left behind to carry the loss. I thought of making an angel magnet with the loved one's name on it. My mom is an artist, so I called her right away and told her my idea. I wanted her to draw and paint the perfect angel for the magnet. I knew then that I had found my calling.

My mom and I always knew we wanted to do something to help others who were walking the same journey as ours. We felt how important it was to reach out to those who are grieving, because each time we did it helped with our own sorrow. So, we began our company, "Inspired To Be," dedicated to creating products that are unique and inspirational. It has been a blessing for us. Our purpose is to help those who are in the stages of grief, and to remind people how important it is to let all of your loved ones know how you feel. All life is precious. Remember to express your love and appreciation to everyone who holds a place in your heart.

My mom and I have also found comfort in helping others through the "Because of Billy Memorial Fund." We started the fund to give help to those in their time of need. Billy will always be there to lend a helping hand, so in his name we give to others because of Billy. We have found that you don't really have to do anything big to give help to others. Compassion and caring go a long way for you and the lives you touch.

I have learned over the years that life changes in an instant, and it goes by very fast. I know that some days all I want to do is to make time stand still and go back to all the precious memories we keep alive in our hearts. I find that I go back moments at a time and remember the life I once knew. I am also grateful for the many blessings that are in my life today. I have my wonderful husband, Michael, my son, Phoenix, my daughter, Destiny and another baby on the way. Even though we walk this journey of loss, we still look for the blessings in our lives. I have so many wonderful people in my life that are now close friends that I have met because of my loss and theirs. I believe we were brought together by our loved ones to help each other to keep moving forward. Blessings are everywhere. I encourage you to look for them. Always remember that there are reasons that you walk your life's path. Find them, and you will find comfort, peace and joy. Listen to your heart. Your life is calling you.

Walk with Faith, Love and Hope in every step.
Live in Love and Give because you can.
Blessings, Angela Michelle Hall

To Honor, To Cherish, To Remember
www.inspiredtobe.com

RICK'S JOURNEY

By Frank Cody

Brenda and I met at work early in 1977. I was the boss and she was a secretary at Channel 100. Channel 100 played current movies on Buckeye Cable via a converter box on your TV. It was a predecessor to HBO, Showtime, and Movie Channel. We became friends at work and started going out with the rest of the crew.

We had great conversations and fun times dancing and listening to music at the local clubs. The Beaver Club was one of our favorites. The house band, "OOPS", played the current favorites. Do you remember "Sunspot Baby", "More Than A Feeling", "Lido Shuffle"?

After a few months of dating, it was time to meet Brenda's children, Jodi and Rick. Jodi was nine, Rick was four. Brenda's description was that Jodi was always the center of attention and Rick, well, he was a non-stop talker. I can remember our evening phone conversations constantly being interrupted by Rick's chattering.

On December 2, 1977, Brenda and I were married before Judge Young at the Lucas County Courthouse. We rented a house in Holland, Ohio, to start our new family's life.

I wasn't sure what to expect as a step-parent. I had read all of the books and articles, and thought that I was well prepared. Little did I know that book training isn't anywhere near the same as on-the-job training. Somehow we managed to endure, from coaching Rick's soccer and baseball teams to attending Jodi's softball and basketball games to summer vacations at our favorite place in the Outer Banks of North Carolina. That is, until the most devastating news of all arrived on Thursday, May 8, 1997. Rick had leukemia at the tender age of twenty-three.

He had not been feeling well for a few weeks, but Rick and leukemia was the farthest thing from everyone's thoughts. And, it was the most aggressive of leukemias, Acute Myelogenous Leukemia (AML). Rick was at work at Pizza Hut when the call came to get to the hospital immediately because a blood test had shown low hemoglobin. He was already receiving a blood transfusion when we arrived at the hospital that evening. His family doctor said that even though Rick had leukemia, it was something from which he could recover. Even though Rick was of slight build, he was one determined individual. The doctor said he had never seen someone that sick who continued to work.

Friday, the family met with the oncologist who also said that Rick was a strong young man, which improved his odds for recovery. That day, Rick received the first of many platelet infusions. Saturday, chemotherapy was started. Rick got through the first round of chemo and was discharged on Friday, June 6.

One paragraph doesn't do the brutal treatment justice. It was six days of two potent chemotherapy drugs. His white blood count eventually dropped to .1. A normal count is 4500 – 10,000. A colony-stimulating agent was used daily to increase WBC production. During this time, Rick experienced temperature swings from 98 – 104 degrees in a matter of minutes. Antibiotics were used, sores developed throughout his body, and he lost his hair. In the end, his body was free of leukemia.

After his discharge, Rick stayed in our Swanton home for a few days. Brenda cleaned his infusion port and Rick built-up his strength. On Tuesday, June 10, Rick went to stay at his apartment with his girlfriend, Jenny and their three-year old daughter, Alexandria. During this time, he went back to work, went on a fishing trip with his father and brother, and spent a lot of time just hanging out with his friends.

On Monday, July 7, Rick returned to the hospital for round two of chemo. It was high dose consolidation therapy for six more days, with some treatments given in triple doses. This concluded on July 15. On July 18, the colony-stimulating agent was started. Rick began experiencing stomach and chest pain and had diarrhea even before his chemotherapy was completed. Because he was not eating, an IV was inserted to continue to administer fluids. The doctors were not concerned about the symptoms because it was a side effect of chemotherapy.

On Saturday, one of the oncologists checked over Rick's now distended stomach. He was concerned about the pain, which was localized in the lower right portion of Rick's abdomen. There was also concern about the possibility of typhilitis, which is an infection of the stomach and bowel lining caused by the chemo. A surgeon was called to examine Rick.

It was eventually determined to insert NG tubes to remove the fluid buildup. This removed some liquid, but it seemed to be a rather small amount. All the while, Rick was getting weaker and had to be helped to the bathroom. Finally, a bedside commode was brought in.

I spent the night of Sunday, July 20 with Rick. I noticed Rick's nurse became concerned about his blood pressure and the fact that there was no fluid coming from the NG tubes.

A new pump was brought into the room because it was determined that the old one was not working. The nurse said she had six other patients to take care of and couldn't spend so much time with one patient. She requested doctor's orders to transfer him to ICU.

Transfer never did arrive. Two CP's (Care Partners) and I wheeled Rick down to SICU. I called Brenda to tell her of the developments. She arrived and stayed in Rick's room. I slept in the waiting room. His condition seemed to stabilize from that on the fourth floor.

On Monday morning, the oncologist arrived around 6:30 a.m. and said Rick was going to need surgery to determine what was going on in his stomach. Brenda would not let Rick go into surgery without being baptized. Rick agreed and the chaplain performed the baptism just before his surgery. The surgery lasted an hour. No damage was found, but there was a sepsis condition. This was deemed a better situation than bowel or intestine damage. After the surgery, Rick was placed on a respirator.

That afternoon, the infection doctor spoke with Jodi and me. She described Rick's condition as poor since there was already evidence of the lungs filling with fluid. She was treating the infection with high-powered antibiotics and expected to see Rick "walk out" of the hospital. To stay close, Brenda and I decided to room at the hotel on the hospital grounds.

By Tuesday, Rick's condition was stable. He was very alert and listened intently as I read an article on the previous night's Red Sox vs. Indians game. He was very responsive to all conversations. Tuesday afternoon, the oncologist met with the family and said that while Rick could die from his condition, there was a good chance that he would survive.

On Wednesday morning at 2:50 a.m., we received a call from Rick's nurse that a couple of changes to his condition had occurred. His heart rate had increased to over 200 beats per minute, and there was blood in his saliva indicating internal bleeding. A half-hour later, we checked back with the nurse, who indicated there was little change except his heart beat was lower from medication. We headed for the SICU and called family and friends to tell of the new developments.

In the SICU, the nurse said the prognosis was not good. The doctor had ordered Vancomycin, which she termed a drug "of last resort". Recovery was deemed unlikely. Based on this information, the chaplain arrived and encouraged us to tell Rick that it was okay to go. The chaplain asked Rick if he wanted the ventilator removed, and if he understood that he could then go to heaven. Rick nodded "yes" to both questions.

The SICU doctor met with us before the ventilator was to be removed. He said that it was his understanding Rick's condition had deteriorated to the point that there was zero chance for recovery and that he agreed with our decision and Rick's approval to remove the ventilator. He said it would take 30 – 45 minutes to reduce the oxygen levels before the tube could be removed. During this time, at least 20 – 25 of Rick's friends and family came in to pay their last respects.

When the ventilator tube was removed, Rick's first words were, "I want to die". He was struggling to talk, but asked about Alex and talked about going to North Carolina. He tried to pull out the IV tubes. He told the chaplain that he wanted them removed. He indicated the same to the nurse. The time was 7:30 a.m. At 8:00 a.m., Rick's primary care physician arrived and began explaining to Rick what would happen if the tubes were removed. Amazingly, the doctor said, "You can still recover from this," and encouraged Rick to reconsider his decision.

We were dumbfounded. The chaplain, the nurse, Brenda and I looked at each other in disbelief. Rick was being told that there was still hope for recovery when an hour before, he had been told there was no chance. I asked the doctor to leave the room to discuss his words. I told him that Rick had made his decision with his family's support. The doctor apologized for not consulting with the family, but said he thought we would want to do everything we could to give Rick a chance to recover including re-inserting the ventilator and cardiac resuscitation.

The SICU doctor called the oncologist to find out what was really going on. The oncologist told me he didn't know where the dire prediction came from, but that there was no organ failure and recovery was imminent if the current course of treatment was maintained. That meant re-inserting the ventilator tube and continuing with the IV's. He said if the situation ever progressed to the point where Rick could not recover, both Rick and the family would be notified.

The chief oncologist scheduled a family meeting for 10:00 a.m. that morning. He began the meeting by saying he didn't know what caused the miscommunication. In his mind, Rick's condition was essentially unchanged. His chances were 50-50 and it was not time to "throw in the towel". In the future, family decisions should be made only after speaking to a member of the oncology team.

I explained that it was our understanding that the nurse's information was the result of speaking with one of the members of his team. Even the SICU doctor agreed with the analysis. The oncologist said that one of two things had happened. 1) The hospital had provided inaccurate information to the on-call oncologist, or 2) The oncologist had made an inaccurate assessment based on the information. He further explained that sometimes the doctors have had a rough night or aren't clear-headed when responding to calls in the middle of the night.

He was to be the sole point of contact anytime there were any questions about Rick's condition. He then told Rick his condition was stable and treatment would continue as before. If ever there was a time when recovery was not possible, both Rick and the family would be notified. Rick nodded that he understood. The rest of the day, Rick remained stable.

On Thursday, July 24 at 3:30 a.m., Rick's nurse called to say he had again taken a turn for the worse. His ventilator and IV settings were at the maximum. We called the family and headed for the SICU. By the time we got there, his condition had stabilized. Later in the morning, Rick tried to bite his ventilator tube and pull it out. To reduce his anxiety, he was given a sedative that the nurse called "Milk of Amnesia". Around 5:00 p.m., one of the oncologists stopped to check on Rick. He said it could take up to two weeks for his marrow to start regenerating and producing a significant amount of white cells.

Friday, July 25 at 7:00 a.m., the nurse called to say Rick's kidneys were failing and his blood pressure was very low. Back to SICU we went. At maximum settings, Rick's blood pressure was too low to attempt dialysis. The chief oncologist arrived and upheld his promise to tell us that now only a miracle could save our son. The family consented that if Rick's heart stopped, there would be no resuscitation attempt. Soon other organs would begin to fail, and eventually there would be brain damage. Around 3:00 p.m., it was time for the family to make a painful decision.

We decided that we did not want Rick to suffer anymore. Our wishes were relayed to the doctor. On his orders, the settings were to be gradually reduced. Rick would feel no pain or discomfort. Rick' ordeal ended peacefully at 3:50 p.m. Fifteen family members and friends were at his bedside.

On Tuesday, July 29, Rick's memorial service was held. My eulogy that day was a tribute to Rick and his devotion to the Boston Red Sox. They were his passion, particularly their All-Star Third Baseman, Wade Boggs. Rick collected virtually everything Boggs—autographed photos, statues, cards, posters, magazine articles. It was all Wade, all the time. But it wasn't just Wade, it was the whole team. I will never forget his joy at having Roger Clemens autograph a baseball at Cleveland Stadium.

Ironically, Rick never attended a game in Fenway Park. He never saw the famed Green Monster or the old-fashioned scoreboard where they still post the scores by hand. He never saw Wade Boggs get five hits in a game or Roger Clemens throw a shutout. I am certain, however, that he had one of the best seats in the house when in 2004 the Red Sox finally won their first World Series in 86 years.

Our tribute to Rick was not yet finished. On Labor Day, 1997, eight family members and friends took the trip to Avon, North Carolina, that Rick was not able to take. At dusk, we all made our way to the fabled lighthouse. There was a brief memorial service with each of us recounting our memories of Rick. Then, we just strolled the beach in silence, scattering his ashes and remembering our beloved son, brother and friend.

Toward the end of the stroll, his sister, Jodi, bent down to pick up a seashell from the shore. Just then, a mighty unseen wave engulfed her. She was soaked. We all laughed heartily. We knew Rick had made it to his favorite resting place.

Saying goodbye was easy. Dealing with the pain of losing a child is a lifetime evolution. Brenda and I knew we needed help, but didn't know where to turn. Somehow, Brenda had heard of a Bereaved Parents Group in Perrysburg. She called to speak with the facilitator. The immediate support was soothing. Brenda wanted us to go to a meeting, which was scheduled for that evening. I was leery, but knew we needed help. A little more than a week after Rick's passing, we were discussing his death with a group of parents who had suffered a similar loss. We had been given membership to a fraternity that no one wants to join.

That first night, there was a lot of anger to be vented; anger at the doctors, anger at God, anger at Rick. No one was spared. The most amazing thing was that the people in the room just listened. They didn't pass judgment, they didn't tell us we would eventually get over the loss, we were not losing our minds, and what we were feeling was okay. This was the start of coping with our loss. As the weeks, months, and years went by, the group provided support that can only be summed up with a heartfelt "Thank You".

If one support group is good, two must be better. This led us to FOCUS. There were some of the same bereaved parents in FOCUS that were in the Perrysburg group, and there were also many new faces. FOCUS was also open to anyone who had lost a loved one. The dynamic is still the same. A loss is a loss. You need to vent, not hold it in. There are no wrong feelings.

Your friendships will change. Some of those you were close with will avoid you like the plague and you will probably lose them. Others you barely knew or did not know at all will become good friends for life. Whatever the case, there is no wrong. You and your friends each deal with death in a different way. Some, like Brenda, me and the bereavement groups talk about it. Others run from it like a contagious disease will attack if they get too close. They can even go as far as to hightail it at breakneck speed to get two aisles away from you at the store when they see you coming.

Then there are the well-meaning who speak about your loss without a clue. How many times have I heard "you will get over it in a few months". If only they knew. You do not "get over it"—ever. You are able to deal with it better, but it never leaves your thoughts. Instead of getting hit with a two-by-four, you are only smacked with a ruler. How about the ones who know, who never mention your child, or those who can't even bear to look you in the eyes. They just look away. This is where the Perrysburg and F.O.C.U.S. groups were a tremendous help. They help you realize that it's not you. Bereaved parents have been dealt a lousy hand that they are trying to make into a better hand. They don't deserve the fate they have been handed.

Then there are the inevitable ambushes. Running into one of Rick's high school friends, passing one of his schools, hearing one of his favorite songs on the radio, finding a photo that you had forgotten existed, passing his favorite restaurant, seeing his favorite movies, *The Shawshank Redemption* or *The Usual Suspects*. His birthday, his date of death, his favorite Christmas holiday, the Red Sox on TV, and, of course, his beloved daughter, Alexandria. While Rick may be briefly out of mind, it is never for long.

One of our treasured memories of Rick came as a total surprise. About a year and a half after his death, one of Rick's best friends presented us with a sketch that depicts how he sees Rick as an angel. It hangs in our home in constant view. The artist captures the essence of Rick. There he is in his t-shirt with the "peace" icon, making the "peace" sign. We often said that Rick was a child of the 60's, living in the 90's. While he liked pop music and modern culture, he was especially drawn to the history and music of the 60's. I'm sure he would have been a hippie.

The sketch shows him with his ever-present Boston Red Sox baseball cap. In his hands are Magic Cards. He loved to play that game. It required a level of strategy and intelligence that he liked to display. He always enjoyed a good challenge. Up in the clouds are angels kicking a soccer ball and hacky sack, just sitting around mellowing out.

The likeness is stunning. Brenda says it is a true "work of heart". It is also rather haunting. Perhaps it's the stark black and white shades. Maybe it's just the constant presence, which is so different from photographs of Rick. It is a brutal reminder of a life taken so young. Maybe it shouldn't be that uncomfortable. Since he is with us every day, why should we not see him at his angelic best? I guess we need to be more accepting of the portrait and take it for what it is—a tribute to the life of our son.

Since Rick's passing, Brenda and I have wanted to honor his life in some manner. Brenda and her friend, Regina Elkhatib, who also lost a son, formed the charitable foundation, "Four The Boys". In their words, the foundation is "to remember Mark and Rick and for those who love them". Through the years, "Four The Boys" has held numerous fundraisers that have raised over $15,000 that was contributed to various children-oriented programs.

For my part, I have continued to donate platelets at the Red Cross. I actually started my donations during Rick's illness, since he needed many infusions of platelets. I have now made over 100 such donations. Every time I do so, I feel I am touching Rick and helping someone else in his honor.

I am also a distance runner. I thought there had to be some way to combine running with doing good in Rick's memory. Three years ago, I found Team In Training, a running program sponsored by the Leukemia and Lymphoma Society. With TNT, you select an honoree (in my case, Rick), select a designated race, train for the race, and raise funds to help fight the diseases. Rick's inspiration has led me to running levels that I never thought I could achieve. I have now completed two marathons for TNT. I have also fostered some great friendships with other TNT runners. Everyone in this support group is participating because these cancers have touched their family or friends. We share our stories and know what we are doing is in some small way helping others.

So, you cope as best you can. Your loss is never out of mind. It may just not always be on the front burner. We will always grieve our loss. If anyone ever says it's time to let go, they may be in danger of a good punch in the nose. They would deserve it. I know Rick is proud of our everlasting love. As I sit here looking at his favorite Red Sox cap, I picture him wearing it on the beach at Cape Hatteras waiting for us to join him.

OUR JAY, JAMIE THOMAS RABARA

By Kathy Rabara

There are so many things about our precious Jamie I don't know where to begin. He was an exciting and interesting child to raise. When I think of him now, I only feel that it was an honor to be a part of his short, but meaningful life.

My second child, Jamie Thomas Rabara began his life in Summerville, South Carolina. He was a healthy little eight-pound boy with a peaceful nature. His older brother, Bill, was three years old when he began his close relationship with his younger sibling. Jay loved Bill, and Bill was a great brother. Jay was close to a year old when we moved from South Carolina to Temperance, Michigan where we still reside. I was pregnant for my third child when we moved. There were only 18 months between Jamie and his newborn sister, Joanna. Little Jamie had to grow up quickly and he proved to be up to the task. Jay had a fierce independent "I do it myself" attitude. He was adored by all his family members, cousins, friends, and neighbors. He had a certain quality that's hard to explain but attracted all kinds of people. His upbringing was pretty "middle class", typical in a suburban area. Jay was always determined and fought for his rights even at a young age. If he knew something wasn't right, he would voice his opinion. He was very intelligent and was sent to school early. He had a spirited but gentle nature.

When Jay was in third grade, I arrived at a conference to find the teacher looking at me puzzlingly, as I said I was there for Jamie Rabara. Oh, she said, "You mean 'Jay' Rabara. Jay told us that you wanted us to call him Jay, not Jamie." After the conference, I confronted Jay and he said, "Mom, Jamie is a girl's name." Later, I learned there was a girl named Jamie in his class.

Jay was a very fun-loving and spirited boy. One quality that he possessed was his fierce determination. His adventurous nature sometimes was unnerving. When he was a young boy, around the age of 12, he swam the entire lake at our cottage with his older cousin, Ryan. We found this out after the fact. Jay was in junior high when he and his friend, Darrin, decided to have their own garage sale while I was at work. He said, "Mom, it was only my junk I was selling!" He was a "handful" to say the least, and this is what made him so interesting, lovable and fun. There was never a dull moment with Jay. He had a great sense of humor and kept our house lively and happy. That was my Jamie Jay; a child with a definite strong personality and a mind of his own.

The teenage years tended to be pretty difficult at first and he did go through a wild stage, but that strong, determined, independent, handsome young man did emerge and shine in his senior year. He was so intelligent, and received one of the top scores for the MEAP test in the State of Michigan. He won an award for this achievement. He was popular at school and was voted president of his marketing class his senior year. He and his father were a lot alike and he inherited that sense of entrepreneurship at an early age. I felt as if he were an "old soul" in a young body in many ways. He had insight to situations, and as I look back, he definitely had a maturity beyond his years.

It hurts to remember some of the confidences he shared with me. He told me once in high school, "Mom, I can see myself married with a couple of kids, but I don't know about the rest of my friends."

Jay cared for everyone and never had anything bad to say about anyone. He wasn't afraid to put himself out and help someone. One night, Jay and his brother, Bill, were driving home when they noticed a car in a ditch. They didn't hesitate to help the driver. It was a woman who had been drinking. Jay and Bill helped carry her out of the car and alerted neighbors to call an ambulance and the police. Another time when he was playing football in a field with friends, one of his friends was making fun of him for not tackling a mentally-challenged kid. Jay had no trouble with that one. He said, "It's not cool to take advantage of someone who is challenged." When only 16, he talked about his girlfriend keeping him on the straight and narrow. I don't know how to explain the enormous amount of wisdom and deep thinking he had for such a young guy. Jay had a heart that was great and caring.

He liked rock and roll music and played a guitar. He even tried to book a band at a local wedding hall. He told me that he didn't think he would ever be in a band, but might want to manage a band for local events. Shining through him was his entrepreneurial spirit.

By the time Jay reached his senior year, he had already gone through the teenage goofing off and he was starting to settle down. We owned a local business at the time, with my husband, Bill, managing a video store in Temperance and I managed one in Lambertville, Michigan. Jay had worked for the stores since he was 14. He was, without a doubt, a great worker. He took it very seriously. He admired his Dad's business savvy and his real desire was to follow in his footsteps as a successful entrepreneur. As president of his marketing class, he set his sights on a scholarship and he was writing a thesis on our family business. My husband recognized his efforts and encouraged him. We were considering opening a third store at the time and Jay was interested in managing it.

Jay really admired his dad. He asked me once, "Mom, what did you see in Dad that you liked so much?" I told him his sense of humor, his intelligence and his honesty. The next day, I heard him on the phone with one of his friends and he said, "Man, you have to get right with school, girls like success!"

Jay had no trouble with girls. He was six foot, two inches tall, good looking, smart, and he really did have that "cool" factor. I remember when he was 15, I purchased a cookie cake with a guitar on it that read, "Happy Birthday Jay 15" on it. He took the 15 off because he was having a girl over that was 16.

Then came the fateful trip his senior year. Jay asked my permission to go to Lansing, Michigan, to visit a friend who attended Baker's College. His friend had been the president of the marketing class the year before and Jay was currently in that position. They were friends beyond school. Jay had a vehicle then, however, it was a typical first-time car for a teenager and not reliable for a long trip. My intuition and some dread come over me. I wasn't comfortable with this idea. I talked with his dad and he wasn't keen on it either. We talked of maybe driving Jay or sending him on a bus. These were decisions we would later regret. Then I came up with an idea that he had to find someone that had a more reliable car. I thought this would squelch Jay's plans, but I should have known better.

As typical with Jay, he did come up with a way. He told me of a boy at school with a newer car that would be willing to take him. The car was a newer sports vehicle. Thinking back, I should have known this would be risky. As parents, we need to be aware of sports-type vehicles and the danger of speeding. It's not just underage drinking and driving that causes many of the highway deaths. This is a decision that I will forever regret, as this was what lead to the end of my precious son's life here on earth.

I was concerned about drinking and driving, so I talked with Jay and the fact that so many kids in college drink. I'd never met this particular friend, so I invited him over for lunch that day and warned them both of the dangers of college drinking. I thought I was covering all the bases with the boys. I warned them not to drink, but if they decided to try a beer to make sure they were not in a car. Jay reassured me by saying, "Mom, it'll be cool. Everything will be all right." Little did I realize these would be some of the last words I would hear from my son. I began to feel uneasy about the arrangements, but shrugged it off.

When the dreaded phone call came in the middle of the night, I dropped to my knees. I've never felt so sick to my stomach and frightened. I couldn't even talk to the police. My husband took over the phone and I could tell in his voice this was bad. We had to drive all the way to Lansing from Temperance which was about an hour and 45 minutes. All I could think of was that Jay's face might be hurt and ruin his looks. At the hospital, I saw him hooked up to all kinds of machines, but he looked okay. I was relieved for the moment. Then the nurses quickly ushered us to a private room and talked with us, however, we couldn't even remember what they said. Next, the doctor took us to a large room and put up x-rays and talked of Jay's brain not functioning. I couldn't bear it and couldn't even look at the x-rays. I felt so sick to my stomach and in shock. All I could think of was despair.

They took Jay to a room and somehow that felt a little hopeful. But then a chaplain came and talked to us to give us the bad news. The chaplain was not very comforting. He kept smiling and saying he understood teenagers. He talked about his own teenage girls. I just tuned him out as it didn't seem like anything I could grab on to. My family was my focus at the time, not his teenage girls. I looked out the window. We were on the second or third floor and I remember thinking how easy it would be for me to end my life. I wanted to die, escape the pain. I know God was hearing my thoughts and he understood. I kept thinking of my family, my Jay. What would my son, Bill, do without his brother? My Joanna would be devastated. And what about my little Timmy? He was so sensitive. Would we survive? I kept thinking that it was up to me to be strong. I wasn't going to give this another thought. I had to be strong or we would all have to commit suicide. This couldn't be happening to us, could it?

Another doctor came in and told us there was no brain activity. Would Jay be a vegetable? I couldn't even grasp this thought. A second chaplain came. This time it was a Catholic priest and he seemed to make more sense to me. He told us Jay had peace on his face when he was in the accident and that he was sure he did not suffer. I couldn't think about it for very long, but now I knew I had to call my family. I just couldn't tell my mother. The first person I thought to call in my family was Marybeth, my sister. She had a special relationship with Jay. She and her husband were living in Alaska at the time and they were planning on giving Jay a trip there for graduation. I called Marybeth and heard her scream "No, no, you can't be saying he's not going to make it!"

Then I saw the window again and I stared. I've never told anyone my real thoughts until now, but I really did think of jumping out that window. I remember silently asking God, "What can I do? How can You help me?" Shortly after this, I know God was with me and took my thoughts to my family, my children, and my husband. They needed me now. My husband made phone calls and took care of other arrangements. My memory is sketchy of this time. I was useless.

My extended family was very supportive and they all rushed to our aid. My brother, John, went over to break the news to the kids that they needed to go up to the hospital. My brother, Pat, and my sister-in-law, Judy, drove the kids all the way up to Lansing without giving it another thought. They also brought their own kids with them, Erin and Ryan. They all loved Jay and were grief-stricken as well. I remember thinking that if I could just go home, this would all go away.

Joanna walked into the room and sobbed and sobbed. Bill was so overwhelmed with grief that he could not hold back tears. Tim was frightened and crying also. It was the first time I ever saw my husband cry out loud. I felt as if I were in the Twilight Zone. I'm not sure of the next events, but I felt the need to stay strong for my family. We eventually took Jay off life support, but I don't remember the details. The only thing I do remember about the hospital was that when they asked for Jay's organs, I couldn't make the decision. Someone else had to decide. I just couldn't think about it.

Our family stayed at a local hotel while they took Jay off life support. This is all hazy to me, but I do remember driving home and that it was the worst drive of our lives. We were all sick to our stomachs. It was awful. When I walked into our house, I felt so uncomfortable. I can't even describe the feeling. Without hesitating, Marybeth purchased an airline ticket and flew home from Alaska to aid our family. My mother, Bill's parents, sister-in-laws, brother-in-laws, siblings, nieces, nephews, friends and neighbors were all there for us taking over all our needs. This meant so much.

Next came the funeral. I replayed it over and over again in my mind. It seemed such a blur and fury of activity. So many people to keep me distracted from the event itself. I wanted to get back at someone, but whom? What could I do with this sick dread in the pit of my stomach? This shock somehow took me through the day's events.

Then began the rest of my life; reinventing myself and our family. It was impossible for months and months to think of anything other than the funeral, the accident, and the hospital. Slowly, however, the reality began to sink in. Shock turned into grief. It overwhelmed my days and gave me restless, sleepless nights. The family kept me going through the day-to-day routine, but I wasn't really living.

It was the "first time" for everything: the first time we ate at the dinner table without Jay, the first time I did laundry without Jay's clothes, the first time I went to school and Jay was not there, the first Christmas, the first birthday, the first winter, the first spring, the first summer, the first fall, the first anniversary, the first graduation, the first wedding, the first grandchild. All these events are joyous, but all were bittersweet. When you're a close family and all are living at home, it was a whole lot of "first times!"

There's no question about it, I was reinventing my existence. For the first few years, I was just surviving, just existing. One of the problems in a grieving family is that everyone grieves differently and everyone is grieving at the same time. Bill, who was the oldest and closest to Jay, truly was inconsolable during the first year. They had shared their lives in every way, and had even double-dated to Cedar Point that last summer. Jay looked at Bill as a great brother whom he could always depend on. They shared a true bond that could never be broken. Bill continued his life but clearly felt grief everyday. When Jay passed, I wondered how Bill would be able to take the loss. He really was lost for awhile. I noticed when entering his room, he would be journaling. Bill was a lesson on how to grieve in your own way. He grieved privately and spent quiet time in his room listening to music. We would talk and he would try to encourage me. I knew his heart was breaking. He was not one to visit Jay's grave. He told me once, "There is nothing we can do to change our reality. We just have to continue." Many times when entering Bill's room, I would find a bible. I knew he was coming to the same conclusion we all were. The answers were with God.

Joanna was a sophomore in high school when the accident occurred. She was caught in the midst of grief and teenage problems all at the same time. She partied to cope with her grief. This became a problem for her later, but I was too deep in grief to really be aware.

Tim was only in junior high school when this happened and he was affected right away with grief. He shared a bedroom with Jay and they used to wake up in the night sometimes and play games. Tim could never bring himself to sleep in that room again. Sometimes I would ride around the block after school with him and we would just talk. We talked about how our lives were changed. Then he'd feel better and we would go on with our daily activities. Soon after, he began the teenage high school years and that's when his partying and wild stage came on. I remember my husband looking at him when he was playing Jay's guitar. He said, "I don't know if I can go through this again." Tim resembled Jay in some ways and it scared us, as he entered his teenage years, with good reason. Let's just say it was like riding a very wild roller coaster. Luckily, the ride didn't last long. Soon after his graduation, things settled down with Tim.

My husband was quiet with his grief like my son, Bill, but you could still see it on his face. I remember thinking, "What we would ever do without Jay?" Nothing was the same. Life was termed "Before Jay" and "After Jay."

One thing that helped me personally on this journey was joining a bereavement group. The group FOCUS, Families Of Children United In Spirit, is for anyone connected to a child's death. I found comfort and friendship in this group and later even helped to facilitate. I believe in support groups, even though I realize they are not for everyone. FOCUS helped me understand my grief, my children's grief, my husband's grief and my friend's and relative's reaction to grieving. It helped me realize everyone grieves differently and that it's pretty common to have many feelings and thoughts. The first few years, I felt as if I were losing my mind. This group helped me realize it was all part of reinventing myself. It's a new life when someone leaves before their time. It's not really a "normal" passing when your child goes before you.

The founders of FOCUS are Mounir and Regina Elkhatib. They lost their precious son, Mark, in a car accident. They are very caring and giving people and have helped all of us who belong. They have inspired us to continue our lives in productive ways in memory of our children. I remember them telling us we must honor our child's legacy in a positive manner. Once I learned this truth, I made up my mind to volunteer in my community and charity events, to work with my PTA, and to become involved with the bereavement group.

I know Jay is safe with our heavenly Father, and that is what comforts me. My faith allows me to cope with my life on an everyday basis. I also know we all have to find our own way. My faith has become front and center in my life. I believe God has a plan for all of us. I'm not sure why bad things happen to good people, but they do happen because of free will. The friend that drove Jay's car was speeding. This was his choice. There are random acts that can cause accidents. We don't always understand why things happen. I believe if you want your child's legacy to stay positive, you have to make a conscious effort to reinvest in life. Jay's life has counted in more ways that I can say.

My husband, Bill, and I testified about Jay's accident to help pass the Graduating Licensing Law for Michigan. The last time I heard, this law is making a difference and saving lives. Bill also helped campaign for the rights of a local bereaved father. We fund a local scholarship at the high school in Jay's name. I volunteer with my FOCUS group as a facilitator. I also help with a bereavement group at my church. Joanna has an appreciation for life and has volunteered with the missions in Haiti. Tim has helped form a church with a friend of his and they minister to the poor. My son, Bill, was so moved by a story where a mother lost her children in a fire, that he sent her money for their funeral. My sister, Marybeth, became a bereavement counselor after Jay's death, and also campaigned for a dying twelve year-old little girl and her mother.

I believe all these events, among others that I have not mentioned, have been done in honor of Jay's passing. In other words, there is gain from this loss. Through the pain, I've grown closer to God and my world. These are the ways we continue. With our faith, we know Jay is safe and we'll be with him in the next world.

It is still hard some days when I think of what Jay lost here on earth. He was truly a gifted, wonderful, handsome, and loving young man with a great sense of humor and caring for others. He made a mark on our hearts that will stay forever. When I feel down and think how he lost his life needlessly, I realize God is faithful. As He promises us in prayer, "He will either shield you from harm and give you unfailing to strength, so be at peace and put all anxiety and fear away."

The lesson I've learned most is that a lot of events and happenings here on earth do not make any sense at all. There accidents, illnesses, murders, crimes, war and poverty. All make little sense in this world we live in. There is only one truth that I can rest in and feel peace. That is the love and peace I get from the Lord. His Word is constant and never changes. He is always there for us to get us through the tough times. A lot of people wonder why God let's bad things happen to good people. Why do war, crime and poverty exist? I can only say that many bad things come from our own free will and choices. Sometimes we are innocent victims of circumstances.

I heard it put this way once. "Life is like a tapestry. When you turn it over, it is full of yarn, twisted and crossed in a mess. When you turn it around, it makes a beautiful picture." I think life here on earth is somewhat the same. There is so much we can't understand, however, when we get to heaven it will all be revealed to us. It's not important for me to make sense of things today, as I know it will be revealed in God's perfect timing.

I feel Jay has left his mark on the world in many ways. I had to reinvent my life to make my son's legacy a positive one. Tragedy can either break you to the point of no return or bring you to a different life with new meaning. I can truthfully say that my perspective is different. Things that used to matter in this world, no longer hold any significance. Most of my friends in FOCUS feel the same way. We hold dear to our hearts, family and friends, and we have a connection to the next world. I've also learned that all people grieve differently to this kind of loss. I never judge people by the way they grieve, as there is no right or wrong way. Some people need to talk constantly. Others need to stay silent. Some people need to journal. Others are unable to write. Some visit the gravesite, while others find no comfort there. We all deserve the right and respect to grieve our own unique way. Just because people don't talk of their loss doesn't mean they aren't grieving privately. Somehow we all emerge different souls, left here without our child, sibling, niece, nephew, or grandchild with a different perspective on what really matters. Many of us go on investing our lives in helping others in a variety of ways. Somehow, we all make it.

All my friends in FOCUS feel we have a little help from above in everything we do here on earth. We live with our loved one's memories in our hearts. They are never far away from us.

JUMPING THE WAKES WITH JACK

By Jodi Hepler

My big brother, Jack had a very adventurous and lively life. I loved every moment I spent with him, good and bad, and I wouldn't give up a second of it. His personality and sense of humor created a lot of who I am. Our sense of humor was so much alike. When he chose to leave us, I felt like he took half of me with him. In our family, he was the only boy in the middle of four girls. He was the one I understood the most. We struggled the most and laughed the most. As much as I begged him not to throw out our life together, he finally took his life by suicide.

I remember the first concern that I ever had of my brother dying was when I was twelve. He would have been sixteen. We took our road trip from Ohio to Fort Lauderdale, as we did every other spring break at my parent's timeshare. We were just three blocks from the ocean in between the intercoastal and A1A. I always loved the spring escape from Ohio. I even helped my brother with his paper route the morning we left so that we could get on the road earlier.

When we finally got there after a long drive, Jack suggested we explore the beach, so we did my sister Robyn, Jack and me. My two older sisters were in college. Jack taught us to fill up a sock with sand and like the dart game, aim them at the washed up jelly fish on the shore and pop them. Gross, but whatever my big brother thought was cool, was always cool to me.

In that same morning, I don't know why, but he decided to go running on the beach without us. I was proud of his sense of fitness and his need to be alone. About an hour or so later, he came limping back. He told me he was just stung by a jelly fish and I could see the red streak going up his leg, poisoning him. He told me to quickly get Mom or Dad. I remember running, crying and begging God, "Please don't let my brother die." I don't remember what happened after that except that he was fine. But for the first time, I actually thought I might lose my brother. That was only the beginning of the many times I worried about losing him because not long after that he started to talk about death and not wanting to be here. I couldn't understand why. We had so much love in our family. I always felt blessed to have the loving family that I had. We were close and unique. To me, I viewed us as being closer than many families I knew.

The real worries started after I came home from being in the Navy for four years. My brother went everywhere I was stationed for a visit, quite welcomed by me. I would actually beg him to visit me. He went to Orlando with my grandparents for boot camp graduation. My grandparents had to be there, of course, since my Grandpa and I were the only ones in my large family that were in the Navy. So Jack came with them to see my graduation and he visited me when I was stationed in Charleston, South Carolina. When my next duty station was Bermuda, I had to have him there to witness the beauty of the island. All of these trips were great and always without any conflict. We just understood each other. That's why I never understood how he could even fathom leaving us as he so often threatened. I thought he was just frustrated and needed our attention since he was the only boy in the middle of a family of girls, but he kept the threats up year after year.

I came home to my parent's house one night with my boyfriend, soon to be my husband, to find Jack passed out drunk on the living room floor with my father's gun that he kept in the safe, pointed at his head. I told my boyfriend to quickly grab the gun and pure rage made me kick Jack in the side. I began screaming, "What the hell are you thinking?" He woke up, of course, and said he didn't know what he was doing. He just didn't want to be here anymore. I just blamed the alcohol, but again, I was so scared of losing him.

That was one of a multitude of threats and scares that he put me and my family through. I will still never understand how he was given such pure, unconditional love by my family and his friends that it wasn't enough to sustain him when he went through his depressed episodes. As his baby sister, I always admired him, loved him, and I was always scared for him.

In high school, he was experimenting with drugs. Our parents were away one night when he threw a party. There were about 20 of his friends there, of course, all stoned. I'm not sure what he took, but it was one of only a few times that I saw my brother cry. He begged me to find his friend, Scotty, or something bad was going to happen to him. I ran around the house yelling to all of his stoned friends that my brother needed Scotty immediately or he might die, or so I thought. They were too far stoned to know what I was talking about. I finally found Scotty, brought him to my brother in the basement. When the two of them saw each other, they just began laughing. I never knew what to predict from my brother. I was only twelve when that happened and from then on it was a constant worry about what might happen to him. I feel as a little sister, that I was groomed to have fun with him then be scared again, constantly back and forth. That was my life with Jack.

He was always quite a lady's man and he never really knew it. Almost all of our girlfriends wanted to date him. He exuded confidence, was always smiling and flirting but internally, he lacked it. I never knew why. He was bright, handsome, funny and not at all arrogant.

I wish I knew how to explain the rest of my life with Jack. The only thing I can say is that I remember more of the happy times than the bad times. I suppose that's normal when you love someone that much, someone that is so troubled. He told me throughout the years about his constant dreams of death and the apocalypse. He would become very disturbed when he had these dreams.

I hope to describe what a wonderful person he was and not apologize for his final action because that action did not constitute who Jack was to all of us. I laughed with him and loved him more often than I pleaded with him not to hurt himself.

In 1987, I began to see the seriousness of Jack's troubled mind. This is when the on and off struggle began with him, and would continue for 19 more years until his death. We were constantly together, going to parties or bars, hanging out at my various apartments, and eventually even sharing an apartment for awhile.

We dreamt and talked about buying a duplex together using my V.A. first-time homeowner's loan. We were very excited about the possibilities. He would live in one apartment and I would live in the other. He loved to paint and fix things, so he would naturally be the caretaker. We hoped to eventually sell after he improved the place and make a profit. But life happened to both of us. He would have a job and then he would lose it. He would have motivation and then he would lose that for months at a time. He drank his way through the good and the bad, and I was there to try to help him get through it all.

My sisters tried as much as they could also, but in stages we all turned our backs on him to show our disapproval, some of us earlier than others. It was our way of trying "tough love" by not speaking to him anymore. My "tough love" treatment just happened to be around two months before my husband and I got married. No conversations, no phone calls, no hugs. This was extremely hard for me to do and it broke my heart. I missed all the laughs, jokes and fun we had. He wasn't working or looking for a job. He was just drinking all day and living at our mother's house after my dad died.

Over those 19 years, when I would talk with Jack, I could always sense it in his voice when his hope was fading, and I would drop everything I had going on at the time to talk to him and get him laughing again and cheer him up. When he would threaten to leave us, he tore me apart. I couldn't understand if we loved him as much as we all did why he didn't love us the same. I spent so many times begging and pleading and playing "the game". I would drink right along with him just so he wasn't alone with his thoughts. I would talk to him for hours and days until I was reassured that he was laughing again and not talking about killing himself. My sister-in-law called me to check on him or talk to him many times when she would start to worry about him. I would come right over to their house and stay with Jack until I was sure we were all laughing again.

Many times when he would get upset, he would head up to our cottage alone. I followed him up there and hung out with him until we both came home laughing and safe. Two times he went up there when he was threatening and upset and I couldn't be up there at that time, so I called the local

153

police to check on him. They were very reluctant without an actual suicide note, which he never did leave. Somehow, I was able to convince them to drive out to the cottage. The police would call me back and say Jack was fine. No matter how much Jack drank, he was always able to pull it together when speaking to the police.

The second and last time I sent the police to check on Jack, they remembered him from the previous time so they put him on the phone with me. In a very detached tone and in a voice that I didn't recognize, Jack just said, "Jodi, you sent them out again didn't you?" I could sense a weak smile in his tone and I just said, "Yes, of course I did Jack, and I always will. Your family is scared and we all miss you." He said he would come home tomorrow. I wasn't satisfied with this because I knew that allowed him one more night alone. He did return home the next day, but he never came back up from his depression. He was just never the same.

I don't know why, but I made a follow-up call to the lake police after Jack died. It wasn't a call in anger, but I just really felt that I needed to let them know that if a family member is sincerely concerned about a potential suicide, it shouldn't be based on whether there is a note or not. With or without a note, they just might mean it. My brother did mean it and was, unfortunately, successful with his threats. I just wanted the police to let their new recruits be aware of this. I hope it made a difference.

I know in my heart that if Jack didn't meet his wife and have his three beautiful children, he would have left us long before. They are the gift he left us to remember what a great man he was. The love and memories I have for him have driven me right into what I needed to do for him and anyone else who feels his pain. I started an "Out of the Darkness Walk" for suicide prevention. He deserved to be honored for the many wonderful things he did for anyone that asked, not dismissed as if his death meant that he didn't matter. He did, to many.

One couple had the audacity to say to my sisters that they didn't know why we were bothering to write an obituary; Jack was going to hell anyway. I can only forgive this kind of ignorance and hope to correct it.

One of my favorite memories of my brother was watching him water ski at our lake in Michigan. Jack skied with total abandon and finesse. He was his happiest when he was skiing, feeling free and jumping from wake to wake or occasionally bare footing, which always amazed us. He absorbed every moment of everyday when his spirits were up, laying under the sun, sleeping under the stars at the lake out on the dock, no pillows, no blankets.

Jack's life was all about music. He introduced me to so many styles, Steely Dan, Moody Blues, Pink Floyd, The Beatles, Bob Marley, Edger Winter, The Doors, Jazz and so many others. It's still hard to listen to the music we listened to together. I expect him to be in the room listening with me. It makes me feel the emptiness so much more.

I remember watching in awe how much he adored his children and wife. I felt that I didn't have to worry about him anymore when I saw him laughing, joking, playing and being totally involved with them. They were everything to him. They corrected everything he felt was wrong about him. The biggest smiles I ever saw on Jack were when he was involved with his wife and children. He taught them to stay up late with him and look at the stars, wake up early and watch the sunrise. He was involved with his daughters in Indian Princess. He loved to teach his son baseball, football and wrestling. He loved dressing up for Halloween and helping with his kid's costumes. He was always laughing, joking and smiling and showed so much pride when he was with his family.

I do know now that in his time here, he was all about absorbing every moment when he wasn't hiding his pain with alcohol or drugs. He was such a loving and caring person. Also, so troubled and none of us know why.

Any survivor of suicide knows we all have our regrets. Among many regrets, my greatest will be the day of my wedding to my second husband, Chip. Chip and my brother were best friends growing up. They were four years older than me. I remember that my husband was one of the few friends of my brother that didn't treat me like the little bratty, tag-along sister. He was always polite and respectful. After I was divorced from my first husband and continued on with my life with my daughter, Sammi, Chip and I reconnected 30 years later out of the blue through a friend of ours. It was great when my brother also reconnected with him.

I knew Jack was happy for me even though life was getting very tough for him. He lost his job, was losing his house and had a wife and three children. When Chip and I decided to get married, we wanted the ceremony to be in a place that made us the happiest, the lake. We wanted only kids in our wedding, including my brother's three children, my daughter, my husband's two children and nephews and their friends. I know my brother was happy for me, but he wasn't happy in general. I didn't share any details of my wedding with him because I didn't want to make him feel bad about his situation at the time. I didn't want to brag about how much better my life was getting. For Jack and me, our biggest common bond was being there for each other and getting each other through our adversities. He would help me; I would help him, usually through laughter. No one has ever been able to make me laugh as hard as Jack did.

As my wedding date got closer, he was emotionally slipping away from us and I was so busy with the plans and getting married at the lake, his favorite place to be, that I wasn't paying attention to the signs. He chose not to go to my wedding, which upset me, his wife, and everyone else involved. The wedding was an hour away from where we live. I was at the lake the night before my wedding and had to go back home to get my hair and makeup done. My intention was to go to his house and pick him up after this because the rest of the family was all at the lake already. Therefore, I was the only one at home where he was without transportation.

Unfortunately, my hairdresser forgot about our appointment. That set me back about 45 minutes and I still had an hour drive back up to the lake. I had every intention of picking Jack up and making sure that he was able to see his beautiful children in my wedding and just enjoy the celebration with all of the family. I felt that he needed to be connected to all of us at this point in his life, noting the level of his depression. I ended up being very rushed and panicked due to the delay. When I was halfway up to the lake, I realized I didn't stop to pick up my brother. I panicked, but I knew if I turned around I would be late for my own wedding. I chose to continue on hoping and believing that he wouldn't miss this and would find someone else to bring him to the lake. He didn't come and it broke my heart. I didn't speak to him the few times I saw him after that. I also didn't hug him, which is something I always did every time I saw him all of our lives.

Two and a half months after Chip and I were married, he had to tell me that my brother just shot himself. I screamed. This couldn't be possible. I just lost my best friend who had been there by my side for everything.

I wish Jack were still here to teach his children to water ski as beautifully as he did. He's not here to see his kids, his pride and joy, graduate, get married, and have children of their own. He won't even know what careers they choose. I know he would be so proud of his oldest daughter, choosing nursing. I know that he set such a great foundation that they will all make the right choices in their lives. I also know that he had tremendous influence on my daughter. As a divorced single mom, he was a wonderful, involved uncle to her. He definitely brought the humor and laughs to all of us.

It took awhile after Jack's death, but I finally joined a support group and got online to find anyone else who had suffered this kind of loss that no one wants to talk about. I found out about the American Foundation for Suicide Prevention. This encouraged me to start our local walk, the "Out of the Darkness Walk." All of the love that I have for my brother continues to drive me to organize these walks. I hope to save a life and support those who have also lost someone they love.

American Foundation for Suicide Prevention
www.afsp.org

JOSHUA

By Sandy Bourland

"We have two children." The words shot from my husband's mouth like a bullet to my heart in response to the car salesman's innocent question. But before he could comment or pose another get-to-know-you-superficially query, I needed to take aim with a few words of my own. "Actually, we have <u>three</u> children." To cover Jim's painful omission, I added, "He and our daughter have been on the outs lately, so I guess he chose not to count her. Twenty-two year-olds can pull some pretty crazy stunts!" My husband just shook his head, with a slight all-knowing smile, probably thinking, "Why do we have to go there?"

It was true, Jim and our daughter, Sarah had not spoken for some time, but that wasn't the "there" to which he referred. He was actually wondering why I couldn't just let his answer go, since the salesman's next obvious questions would've been, "How old?" or "Girls, boys, or one of each?" And then, it would've been simple. "Our daughter is 22, and our son is, 17." If he'd answered that we have three children, "Son, forever 18," he would have had to come up with an explanation. Talking about Josh's death, nearly seven years ago, to a stranger . . . what did it matter? And, really, why do I always need to go "there"?

I can't for a moment, not even to a stranger in a once-only conversation, fail to acknowledge my son, Joshua. It feels wrong. I know my husband, Jim, Josh's dad, disagrees. He is a concise, in-control (shall I say "typical"?) man who reserves the pain and joy of talking about our son with those who matter to him. Strangers don't count—don't get into it, period. And do I believe that either of us loved Josh more, or less, to result in our differences? No. But, we certainly handle his death differently.

At one point, in the second hospital ER unit where Jim and I huddled together, stunned, I thought of how we were the only two people who knew what it felt like the moment Josh was born and what a bond that had been for us. Now, we were bonded again by his death. How could anyone else ever know how it felt to let go of our beloved son? How wrong I was to think being parents to the same child binds you! Grief is such an individual, personal, visceral process. It feels like "It's every man for himself!" You can support each other by talking, holding, yelling and just being there for each other. But your path is your own, one which you must walk in solitude, shaded by the relationship and experiences that you, alone, shared with your child.

Joshua James Bourland was born on March 13, 1982 at 5:32 p.m., our first child. We were young and so thrilled to be blessed with such a perfect gift, although bald and cone-headed! Being the first grandchild on either side meant that a whole host of relatives eagerly awaited his arrival, literally; they overflowed from the waiting rooms! For two and a half years, Josh was doted on—from hand-painted art and lovingly crafted bedding and toys in his nursery to original outfits, sewn and knitted with affection. Jim and I refused to put him on a schedule because putting Josh to bed early at night meant less time to play with him. He was happy and so were we; and that was all that mattered. We had fun!

When his sister, Sarah, was born just before Josh turned three, nothing much changed. Now, there were two beautiful kids to spoil and enjoy—and did we ever! The four of us became the family Jim and I had long dreamed about. Housework and home improvement could wait, because enjoying these kids and seeing the world through their eyes was our top priority! Josh always looked out for his little sister, and they were the best of buddies, at least until the dolls came out. Josh was happy to play all day, fostering Sarah's inner tomboy, but drew the line at baby dolls and Barbies, much preferring his He Man characters!

So, after five years of a very "balanced" family with one girl and one boy, Josh got the brother he'd secretly hoped for! Chaos arrived with the name of Carter. Probably, but not scientifically proven, he was the result of pregnancy cravings for ultra hot salsa and chili dogs with hot peppers!

Instantly nicknamed "Little Viking" for his stubborn streak and strength, this baby was given his proper name by his older, wiser brother, Joshua, who proudly deemed him "Carter" in honor of his favorite New York Mets catcher, Gary Carter. It stuck! Josh was so proud to have named his little brother, he set out to teach him all he knew that was boy. Little Carter found everything that big Josh did to be instantly cool. They watched so many baseball games together that Josh had Carter catching with a mitt at age two. This was a kid who went from infancy to thinking he was ten years old in a blink! He never wore cute baby clothes; he had to wear giant sports t-shirts and giant caps that were "real", like Josh's.

Everything that Josh did, he tried to include Carter. He was a mentor before the word caught on, never realizing how much he was actually teaching by example. Whether playing Home Run Derby or roller hockey, the rule was that Carter had to be allowed to play, by Josh's decree, and had to play tough, like the big boys. If he cried or couldn't handle it, he was out. Of course, Carter was always protected by his big brother, who was athletic and coordinated enough to play and oversee him simultaneously. And since Josh was so well-respected and liked by his friends, no one ever complained about including his little brother in their games. And nobody else had a little brother who was tough enough and talented enough to play! But how did that happen? Having Josh for a big brother is how. As a result, Carter grew up with the confidence that comes with acceptance and kick-ass sports skills!

Do we ever know how happy we really are at any given time in our lives? I don't think so. At least I don't think I realized how wonderful and blissfully normal our family was as our children were growing up. I was a busy working mom with three lively kids who were involved in a multitude of activities. In fact, I recall complaining about my lack of time quite often. Now, I'd give anything to have that wondrously hectic, hurly-burly time back again.

Time passed quickly for our family. Josh and Sarah had forged a new relationship as teenagers, sharing private jokes and keeping each other's secrets. As the consummate big brother, Josh screened Sarah's potential boyfriends, finding only one worthy of her attention. He provided the wheels for trips to the mall, movies, friends' houses and other favorite hangouts for Sarah and her pals. After turning eighteen and graduating, Josh made the decision to stay at home and attend the University of Toledo, halfheartedly pursuing an engineering degree but fully involved with his friends. Sarah was busy and talented at sixteen, balancing dance instruction and performance with a full social life in high school. Carter, at ten, lived for AAA hockey which put us in Detroit five to six times a week and out of town or country a few weekends each month. Things were going well, like they were supposed to, as Jim and I had been taught. If you had faith, paid your taxes, lived within the law, and were active, loving parents, life would all go as planned until you were reminiscing about the "good old days" with your grandchildren around a Thanksgiving table. Right.

On December 5, 2000, as Sarah and I began our annual Christmas decorating blitz, the phone rang. Life, as our family had known it, was over. Joshua had been involved in a serious automobile accident. Although nearly seven years have passed, I cannot bring myself to recount the specific details of this experience. It has taken the flashbacks and night sweats of Post Traumatic Stress Disorder to assimilate the vivid images into my conscious memory. All I can share is that I was stoic and calm—qualities never before associated with me—as I phoned a friend to drive Sarah and me the 25 minutes to the hospital and called my husband, at his office an hour away, to join us. By the time Josh was Life Flighted back to our local hospital, St. Vincent's, a large group of family and friends had gathered to be at his side. It was this wonderful collective who helped us pick up the pieces of our shattered family and put it back together in its new, yet horribly-altered state.

The accident surely claimed Josh's life upon impact at 6:32 p.m., yet he was not pronounced until 11:45 p.m. That night seemed endless, but in reality was only a taste of the never-ending pain of his loss. It took Jim and me over three years to resolve criminal and civil proceedings against the friend of Josh who was driving that night and to settle Josh's estate. Who knows that an eighteen year-old college kid needs a will? We do, now. And we know an awful lot of things about the legal system we'd never wanted to learn.

But we also learned things that we cherish. We are deeply gratified to know how much Joshua meant to so many people, many of whom we did not even know. From the cards, letters, phone calls and visits we received to the testimonies of those who rose to speak from the heart at Josh's memorial service, we came to understand how his life positively impacted the lives of so many people besides our own. We also know that life isn't measured only in years, but in the good that it brings to others. And we know that Joshua remains with us, by our sides in spirit and in our hearts and minds through memories, and that we will most certainly be with him again one day.

Jim, Sarah, Carter, and I will continue to cherish and share our collective memories of Joshua, yet we will each hold fast to our private remembrances which guide and shape our individual loss. Each of us has been profoundly affected by Josh's death in our own unique manner, and life continues to hold challenges as these effects surface. We've each been forever changed by Josh's death, yet, most importantly, each of us has been individually touched because of his life. And for that reason alone, I will always proudly say, "I have <u>three</u> children."

FORGIVENESS

In Memory of Patricia Diehl

By Carol L. Plenzler

My story begins on a warm, sunny day in June, 1997. My husband, Ron and I were working in the yard using the leaf blower and mowing grass so we didn't hear the sirens less than a mile away. To my surprise, one of our parish priests pulled up into our driveway. We are very active at St. Clement Church so I thought nothing of Father being there. I took him out back calling Ron to our back porch. I went to leave, as I thought he wished to speak to Ron privately. He said, "Carol, I want to talk to you also. There's been an accident." I asked immediately if Pat were okay. He said, "No, she is with God." If you could have hit me in the chest with a two-by-four, it couldn't have hurt more. We all stood crying. I thought my head would explode!

The story we were told was a young man had been driving erratically down the road my sister lived on. My sister was walking home from the store when a van jumped the curb, hitting her with such force it threw her 80 feet and out of her tied shoes. Her body hit a telephone pole landing within four feet from a basement apartment window. She died at the scene of a broken neck and blunt force injuries.

I was told at the funeral home by well-meaning friends and clergy that I had to forgive this man. I said, "I will never forgive him for ripping my sister out of our lives as he did."

After seven months of going twice a week down to the Lucas County Court House, I finally saw this man taken out in cuffs. I thought I'd feel good about this, but I didn't. He was sent to prison for four years on February 17, 1998.

Ron and I were told of a Cursillo in Carey, Ohio in March, 1998. Ron decided to attend the men's Cursillo. I reluctantly agreed to go to the women's Cursillo in May. I was so angry and hurt by the senseless death of my sister. Why did God allow this to happen to her? Upon arriving that Thursday evening, I really did not want this "God thing" everyone was so excited about. To my amazement, by Saturday I finally realized my God loves me so very much and had died so we could all go to heaven. While hanging on the cross, He said "Father forgive them for they know not what they do!" If He can forgive these men, why can't I forgive Fred, the man who hit my sister?

After a year of a lot of prayer and counseling, in the early hours of Valentine's Day, I was able to sit at my desk and write to Fred. I told him, "I forgive you, but I will never forget what you did to my family. I hope while you are there you get your GED and some counseling." I mentioned I'd like to hear from him as to how he is doing. About three months later a letter arrived from Ross Correctional in Chillicothe, Ohio. I was afraid to open the letter not knowing what he had to say to me. While sitting on our steps, I got the courage to read the letter. After reading it, I began to cry. What he said to me was from the heart. He was unable to forgive himself for what he did.

I told him in another letter that God forgave him a long time ago. He needs to forgive himself.

During that time, I became involved in MADD (Mothers Against Drunk Driving) and have given talks at DIP programs (Driver Intervention Program) to educate the defendants on the dangers of drinking and driving.

The last time I saw Fred was when he was sent to prison seven years ago. Now he was free and I found out he was arrested for a DUI and would be at a DUI program where I speak regularly. I was notified by one of the counselors that Fred would be there the next day when I was to talk. I had never been able to speak to him face to face to let him know the pain he had caused.

I gave my talk as I always do. I tell my story, how it has affected me and so on. As my talk started, he laid his head onto his arms and sobbed. When my talk was over I went to him and called his name. As he looked up I hugged him and I said again "I forgave you and so has God. You need to forgive yourself." As I held him in my arms, through his tears he said, "I am so sorry! I am so sorry!" As we were hugging, I felt the power of God's love. My prayers were finally answered. I was able to hold him and feel his pain and tell him that God loves him so much!

We don't understand why some things are allowed to happen. God wants us to remember, if we forgive, healing is on its way regardless of whether it's physical, emotional, or spiritual. God knows when we're hurting and wants to feel that hurt. Remember, forgiveness and healing of memories brings peace of mind and heart.

When we were cleaning out Pat's apartment, we found she loved butterflies! There will be many times before I give a talk that I will see a butterfly somewhere and know her spirit is with me. This gives me the strength to give my talk without any problems. I feel a great peace come over me.

As a result of my sister's death, I have become a stronger and more focused person, living everyday enjoying the gift we have all been given—life.

BENJAMIN

By Teri Bowden

My name is Teri Bowden. I have been married for eighteen years to Danny Bowden. We have three children, Christina, Derick (my step son), and Benjamin, the youngest. We were a typical family, busy with life and going through the motions. I worked as a cashier and my husband was a truck driver. I have always been very active in my children's lives. I went to school functions and helped with homework. We had four dogs and two cats. I dusted every week and vacuumed everyday. We were consumed with the everyday business of life.

I have always been a positive person, looking for the good in people and in life. I told everyone how blessed and fortunate I was. I truly meant it. Don't get me wrong. My life was not perfect. We didn't always have everything we wanted, but we had all we needed. We also had the typical teenager problems. Christina wanted to be treated like an adult, but also wanted the benefits of being a child. Benjamin wanted to see how far the boundaries could be stretched. We also had the stress of my husband being on the road.

In our family, I was the take-charge, fix-it person. I was the one who knew how to take care of everything. I always thought I could control the situation and the outcome. It was a really nice fantasy to think I had that much power in the world. I was soon to realize just how little control I had. I think that was one of the first hard lessons I learned. My husband was, and still is, the rock of the family. He was away from home a lot. When he was home, he was always working on a project of some sort. Even with his frequent absences, he stayed very active in our daily lives. Thank goodness for cell phones!

My daughter, Christina, has always had a strong personality. She knew what she wanted and when. Even now, the older she gets, the more proud of her I become. She still likes her alone time and her privacy. I have learned to respect her. My son, Benjamin, was a very social person. He had many friends and loved being with everyone. He smiled and joked a lot. He got that from his dad.

Benjamin was born on June 28, 1989. When he was just a baby, I dreamed of his death. I couldn't see how old he was, but it was a very vivid dream. Because of that dream, I was a bit over protective of him. He was the oldest one at the beach wearing a life jacket. He went to the doctor at the first sign of an illness. He was in the driver's training as soon as it was legally allowed. I wanted him to have tons of driving experience before he went out on his own.

Both of my children had a nasty habit of breaking and spraining their right ankles. One Christmas, both were in casts and on crutches. They had broken their ankles one day apart from each other. I think the rest of the family almost broke their necks that year tripping over all of those crutches! Benjamin had ankle surgery his junior year of high school. It had to be timed just right. Surgery had to be after football and not interfere with wrestling. Benjamin had to be healed before his senior year of football. The surgery went well. He hated not being able to drive, but it didn't slow him down. He went out with his friends on Friday and Saturday nights. He still went to wrestling meets and even went to the State

Tournament with the team on his crutches. I begged Benjamin to go to prom his junior year. He kept saying that he wasn't going. He said he would go his senior year. At the last minute, he asked his girlfriend to go to her senior prom. So, the hunt for the perfect tux began. He was very picky, but eventually we found what he was looking for. Things were good. He borrowed his grandfather's Corvette to drive that night. He had a great time!

May 25, 2006, my life changed forever. It was a Thursday just like every other Thursday. I was at work and the kids were at school. Benjamin came home afterward and asked what was for dinner. I said, "McDonalds." He said, "I'm tired of McDonalds." I told him I would give him money for something else. He was going to his girlfriend's high school graduation, so he said he would pick up something on the way. He went to her graduation and then out to dinner with her and her parents. I called and talked to him at 10:20p.m. He said he was just leaving to come home. I told him I loved him and that I would see him soon. When he wasn't home at 11:00 p.m., I called his cell phone. It went to voicemail. I was starting to get worried and a little angry. It was a school night and his driver's license was only good until midnight. At 11:30 p.m. I called his girlfriend. She said he had left fifteen minutes earlier. I wanted to feel relieved, but I didn't. Something just didn't feel right. I was sitting on the couch thinking maybe I should drive the road between our house and hers. Maybe his car had broken down.

I know this will sound crazy, but I have to say what I felt that night. I started talking to a family friend who had died. I asked them to please take care of Benjamin on his drive home. The response I got was, "You don't have to worry about him. He is here with me." I cried for a minute and then felt a sense of calm. I took a shower and got dressed. I turned the front porch light on. Around 1:15 a.m., I heard a car pull up to the curb out front. I heard two car doors shut. A police car has a distinctive sound. I'll never forget it. I was sitting on the couch as the two state police officers walked up to the porch. I saw them take off their hats, and watched them knock on the door. They knocked a second time. I went to the door and told them to put their hats back on. I said, "He's just hurt, right?" "No ma'am. Who can we call for you?" they asked. I told them it really wasn't a good time. My husband was out of town fourteen hours away, and my father-in-law was on a motorcycle trip. I told them that it was a holiday weekend, so Benjamin had to just be hurt. They told me that he had died instantly at 10:56 p.m. I asked if anyone else was hurt. They said no, but that there was another vehicle involved. The semi truck driver was okay, but was shaken up very badly. Again, they asked whom they could call. I called my family friend, Terry.

I called Danny and told him he needed to come home. I told him there had been an accident and to drive carefully. I told him that I didn't need two of them in the hospital to take care of. I was trying to find a way to get him home without finding out that his son was dead. I needed him to be safe. My sister-in-law and Derick went to get Christina from work. They had to take the back way because the main road was still closed due to Benjamin's accident eight hours earlier. I know I wasn't there in the way my daughter needed me to be, but I did the best I could. My husband arrived home at 2:00 p.m. the following day. His first words were, "I'm so sorry." He told me that no matter what had happened he didn't want to lose me also.

I remember everyone telling me what to do, what to eat, when to sleep, when to shower and not allowing me to answer my own phone. I got really angry and I told them that I would eat and sleep when I wanted to. My mom wanted to do the dishes. When I told her not to, she and my mother-in-law did them anyway. I was so angry because that was Benjamin's chore. I remember family members writing his obituary. When I wanted it worded a certain way, I was told that was not how it was done. I went outside and said, "I don't know why I'm here! He's my son, but what I want doesn't matter! Just let them plan the whole damned funeral!" That is when my husband stepped in and told a family friend what was happening to me. Danny said that he didn't care, but that I was to be made to feel in charge of my son's funeral event even if I wasn't. No one meant to hurt me, they were trying to help me.

The day after the accident, my sister-in-law and brother went to the impound lot to gather Benjamin's belongings. They had to get permission from the state police and the towing company had to stand there and watch them go through my son's things. They were able to get several bags of his clothes, his cell phone and his I-Pod before they got damaged in the elements. They also took pictures of the damaged car. These were cherished possessions. We still have his cell phone turned on. I like to call and hear his voice. My sister-in-law also took my daughter shopping for a dress for the funeral. She replaced his cologne that had been broken in the car so I could have that smell. My sister-in-law stepped in to help Christina when I just could not be there for her.

The planning of Benjamin's funeral began the next day. We picked out a casket, a vault . . . all the normal things I never planned on needing for my sixteen-year, ten-month, and twenty-five day old son. The funeral director was wonderful. He had us bring in all of Benjamin's favorite things. We brought his football helmet, roller blades, hockey stick, guns, and stuffed animals to the funeral home. Basically, his room was moved to the mortuary. I then went and bought him a new shirt to wear and the shoes we had to put on hold the night before he died. The funeral director then gave me the earring Benjamin was wearing. It was one of my diamond studs. The other one was lost at the accident scene.

I planned my son's funeral to be a comfort to his friends. There were books where they could write funny stories about Benjamin. Adults were not allowed to read their stories. There were paper and envelopes so his friends could write letters to him and put them in the casket. These were kept private. The kids made CD's of his favorite music. By taking care of his friends, I had a focus. The stories these kids wrote have become a favorite past-time of mine to read. I read and reread them. I can now blackmail most of the kids in our town. I joke and say that if Benjamin were here, he'd be, oh, so grounded. Some of the money envelopes got confused with the story envelopes that were going into the casket. I know Benjamin just loved it that he took money with him.

We did not get to see Benjamin until the viewing at the funeral home. I didn't know I could go to the hospital to see him. This is one of my biggest regrets. The service was held at a local church and Benjamin's pastor presided. We brought his favorite blankets to tuck him in before we closed the casket. There were so many people. They were everywhere, even standing outside when the church filled up. I felt so guilty that I couldn't speak to everyone. After the graveside service, his best friends stayed behind. They were the ones to bury him. The cemetery sexton at one time had been their baseball coach. He allowed them this last way to honor their friend.

My sister-in-law had asked my permission to take pictures of the funeral. I'm so glad that I have them now to remember the last moments with my son. That isn't something that is commonly done where we live, and it did raise some eyebrows. We designed Benjamin's headstone and were present for the pouring of the foundation and for the setting of the headstone. Benjamin's birthday was the following month. My niece wanted to have a picnic in the cemetery. We had pizza and cake. All of Benjamin's friends showed up, so we took a road trip to his favorite restaurant, Hooters. At Halloween, we carved pumpkins. At Christmas, Benjamin had a tree complete with lights and ornaments. We had balloon releases. We also threw barbecues and brought things to the cemetery that reminded us of Benjamin. We light candles at the cemetery and at home for special events. I see the light of the candle as the light of Benjamin's smile.

Benjamin's car was impounded for about seven months. In the first month, I went there several times either with someone or alone. I also went there with Danny. We were able to get the beads from a broken necklace and some other minor things that now mean the world to me. The tow truck personnel were so nice and even helped sort through the shards of glass for some beads. I wanted to find the missing diamond stud earring. Not only was it mine, but Benjamin had been wearing it during the accident. The tow truck driver was trying to be so helpful. He was gently telling me that we had recovered more personal belongings than most, and how lucky we were. There were days I would stop in and just say "Hi" to the driver. I guess I wanted to be close to Benjamin. After all, his car had been the last place he was alive, and he died in that car alone without me. It didn't seem fair that Benjamin should die without me being there. I was there for his birth and all of the important events in his life. Why wasn't I there for his death?

The third-month anniversary of Benjamin's death was also our sixteenth wedding anniversary. We decided to go to the car again. I sat in the driver's seat of the car. Danny and the tow truck driver told me not to because of the broken glass. I needed that connection. I ignored them. I NEEDED to sit there and feel my son. I can't even tell you what they were doing, but I was just silently talking to my son. I started digging through the glass in what used to be the bottom of the driver's door.

While listening once again to Danny warning me that I was going to cut myself, I found my earring. It was slightly bent and weather beaten. I felt it was a sign from Benjamin that he was okay. I also felt it was a message to stop coming to the damn car! He knew I would be persistent. I could never stand not being able to find a lost item. Now I wear one earring and my husband has his ear pierced and wears the other.

We have been to the accident scene many times. I sometimes sit there and talk to Benjamin. On my way to work I must pass the site, so I needed to be able to go there and find comfort. It took time, but now I can go on that stretch of road and honk or play a favorite song of his really loud. Danny and I now carry pieces of Benjamin's car in our pockets.

I am the type of person who needs to know everything. I have the police reports, the accident scene pictures, and the medical examiner's report. I keep these in a lock box. Danny has no interest in these things. I find myself looking at them occasionally. Since Benjamin died, I have had to battle panic attacks, insomnia, and have developed some obsessive-compulsive behaviors. I have a hard time leaving his possessions at home. I am afraid that I will lose what I have left of my son. Medication has helped with some of these problems. I also go to counseling, have an online support group, and attend a bereavement support group called "F.O.C.U.S." I have discovered it is important to me that I find something outside of myself that helps me cope.

Benjamin's death has taken a toll on my marriage, as well. No two people grieve the same way. For the first time in our lives together, Danny and I needed different things. I wanted to see Benjamin's car. Danny did not. He wanted to order the headstone right away. I needed time. We had lost the same person, but we were not in the same place. How do you determine whose needs are more important? It's hard to find a way to balance each others' needs. We started to do things alone and it seemed like we just couldn't talk to each other. For the first time, we were drifting apart with no sense of connection. Neither one of us had the energy to even think about how to fix what seemed broken.

On top of this, money became, and still is, an issue. I could not go back to work, and Danny couldn't work the long hours with weeks away from home like he had been doing before Benjamin died. Now we are struggling to keep our house. One day, we were sitting on the couch and I asked Danny what he was thinking. "Nothing", he responded. It hit me that we were no longer together; we were just living in the same house. I told him how I felt, and we began something new. Every night now, we pick a topic (silly or serious) to talk about for ten minutes. This is how I discovered that my husband hated spaghetti. I had been feeding him spaghetti once a week for sixteen years! He ate it without ever telling me. Our marriage has now become stronger than ever. We still have bumps, but we make a conscious effort to stay connected. We are still having money issues, but we do still love each other.

I have watched how society and our friends and family seem to treat me and my husband differently. They feel his grief is not as bad as mine, and he is supposed to take care of everything. They expect him to be stronger and to pick up the pieces faster than me. I think this is so unfair to grieving fathers. Danny has had a very hard time. Not only did his son die, but I am no longer the wife I used to be. Danny now spends a lot of time alone. I went from a take-charge person, to someone who didn't even remember to shower unless I was told to. I no longer paid the bills or went to the grocery store. I was incapable of making a decision. I was afraid I would be wrong. I have gotten better, but I do weigh things more now, before deciding on anything. I have to take notes so I don't forget appointments.

There are so many landmines in grief. The first time I went to the grocery store, I was so surprised at my reaction. There was the last thing I cooked. There was the food Benjamin liked to eat. There was the food he hated. I expected certain things to be hard, but I always find some shocking surprises that sneak up on me. When I go to events or to a friend's house, I never know how long I will be able to stay. It might only be measured in minutes or it could be hours. It's nothing personal, it's just that seeing people happy sometimes really hurts. I remember in the beginning thinking how people could go on with their lives. My baby isn't here anymore. Haven't you noticed that the sun doesn't shine anymore? The world should just stop.

One of the really surprising things that happened to Danny and me was that the people who were close friends just disappeared. Others came forward in their place. We found that many people just couldn't handle seeing us anymore. One friend said that she felt so guilty because she was so very sad Benjamin had died, but so glad it wasn't her child. The guilt of that feeling keeps her away. To some, we are their worst nightmare. We are a reminder that the death of a child can, and does, happen. I have learned that most people mean well. When they say "stupid" things, it is not their intention to be hurtful. They just don't know what to say. I hate the, "You are so strong! If it were me . . ." I feel that means they love their children more than I loved mine because they couldn't live without theirs. Trust me. It's a daily, sometimes hourly, struggle to remain on this earth. Another favorite is, "You have other children, right?" This assumes that I could replace Benjamin. Once, my husband leaned over to me after someone had made such a comment and whispered, "They should have just sent a card."

Within a month of Benjamin's death, I went to the cemetery. I just knew if I could see and hold him one more time, I would be okay. I decided that was just what I was going to do. I looked around for a shovel. Not finding one, I went home and got one. When I returned to Benjamin's gravesite, I dug a few holes when I realized what I was doing. I immediately stopped. My mind has played tricks on me. It doesn't seem to always register his passing. Sometimes I think, "When he gets home from school (or camp, etc.), I am going to tell him . . . I will be driving and remember I need to remind Benjamin of something else. Then it hits me. He won't be home to tell anything to. Regardless, I do talk to him all the time.

When your child dies, nothing in your world stays the same. It changes your view on your entire life. Dusting and vacuuming are no longer a priority. I have said that when Benjamin died, I didn't want to become a bitter, old woman. I try to make someone smile everyday to honor him. I'm still trying to be a positive person, but it isn't as easy as before. Where people see joy, I see possible heartache. When someone says that there is only a one-in-a million chance that something could go wrong, I plan for that chance. I now see the world in terms of danger.

Just recently, my daughter and daughter-in-law both had babies. Now I am a grandma. During their pregnancies, I was so worried about something happening to them in childbirth, or the babies having problems. They are both perfectly healthy. Now that they have arrived, however, I worry about SIDS. I think how I couldn't protect my own son, so how am I going to protect my grandsons? Losing a child changes how you think.

I now call those who have not lost a child, the "normal people." They still view life like the old me. I now have an unusual sense of humor. The first year after Benjamin's death, we decided to go to Florida on Christmas day. We were leaving the cemetery and I was crying because I did not want to leave Benjamin. Danny said, "Teri, think of it like this. It's the first time he will be exactly where he's supposed to be, doing what he is supposed to be doing." I just started laughing.

Things in life are now so trivial. In that way, my life is so much better than before. Now I don't take people for granted. I would rather spend time with those I love than with those I don't. Housework is not important. If you come to my house to see me and don't like my messy home, we'd better meet somewhere else. I listen to people complain about their children and think how minor these things are. I went to several football games after Benjamin was gone to support his best friends. One of the parents said to me, "Why are you here? You don't have to come anymore." She acted like that was a good thing. Once, a parent was complaining very loudly to the athletic director about her son not playing. She said that she didn't want to come to the games to watch her son stand on the sidelines. Very quietly I said, "I would do anything to see my son on the sidelines." She looked at me and just got quiet. She apologized and left. We have all learned what is truly important in our lives. The new me likes that.

I have had multiple losses in the past three years. My aunt passed in September of 2005, my son passed in May of 2006, and then another aunt passed in June of 2007. My mom then died on December 24, 2007 and my grandma died in April of 2008. Each loss affected who I was and how I thought. I feel I still haven't grieved for my mom and grandma. I'm still focused on Benjamin's death.

I believe we are put on this earth with a mission to complete and when our mission is fulfilled, we go home to God. I think Benjamin is what some would call an old soul. He was here to help others spiritually. His death will help me find my path with my own mission in this life. I have heard stories from people about Benjamin that have led me to believe this.

As seasonal campers, we've become close to other families at the campgrounds. When Benjamin was about fourteen, he was walking on of the trails and he came upon a lady who was crying. He sat down next to her and asked her what was wrong. She had breast cancer. She was scared. Benjamin told her it would be okay and asked if he could hug her. My son gave the best hugs. You could feel them from your head to your toes.

The school custodian's niece had been in a severe car accident. Benjamin asked about her every time he saw the custodian. No matter what was wrong in their day, he would always listen to his friends and make them laugh. I did not go to church regularly; however, my son went with the neighbors. When he got his driver's license, he drove himself. If he spent the night at a friend's house, he would get up and go to church. He never made a big deal of it, or even told his friends where he was going. He just went. I was astonished when I was told stories about my son. I was happy to know he touched so many lives in is short life. My son's life and death have been full of lessons for so many. I now know seventeen year-olds who tell people they love them, and that Benjamin's death taught them not to take people and things for granted. Sometimes I get angry that my son is not here and people are here who hurt and steal from others. That's when I think to myself that Benjamin's mission was completed. That is why he went home to God. That thought doesn't take the pain away, but it does dull it.

The guilt and the "what ifs" can eat me alive. I now know it is normal to have these thoughts. I just have to find a way to control them. In the beginning, I thought if I had made Benjamin dinner, or if I hadn't let him go to his girlfriend's graduation, then maybe this wouldn't have happened. After all, he was grounded for not cleaning his room. But, then I came to believe that when it's your time, it's your time. If I hadn't let Benjamin go out that night, maybe he would have fallen down the steps. Maybe he would have died some other way. I have also wished I would have changed or done some things differently. I battle regrets. Why didn't I let him buy that dirt bike or snowmobile? There are a million things I could have done differently. With time, I realized this would not have changed the outcome. As a parent, I did the best I could. I read somewhere that if you die in a traumatic way God takes you in his arms before your actual death. I like that thought and it gives me comfort that Benjamin wasn't alone and scared. I used to dream and would remember them. Since Benjamin's death, I no longer do. I miss dreaming and hope one day they will return.

Sometimes I feel Benjamin around me and get a smell of his cologne. Not how it smells in the bottle, but how it smells when it mixes with someone's own unique scent. I see shadows that I know are him. The dogs will play with him and watch him. I know Benjamin is there when they do the little "play bark" they always did with him. Benjamin is with my husband a lot as well. He likes to play little tricks on him. He will knock things over in the truck continuously until Danny says, "Benjamin, enough." At home, Danny has heard things fall in Benjamin's room, but when he goes in there, nothing is out of place. Danny just says, "Benjamin, did you find what you were looking for?!" The new grandbabies stare and smile. They move their little hands like they are playing with someone. I am sure it is Uncle Benjamin. I show my grandbabies his pictures and tell them stories about their uncle and grandma.

I measure time differently. Now it's "before Benjamin died" and "after Benjamin died." Benjamin's friends have been so wonderful. They are not afraid to say his name. They are not afraid to cry in front of us. We are not afraid to cry with them. They don't put a timeline on our grief. Twenty-nine months after his death, his friends still call and visit. Most importantly, they still let me be Benjamin's mom.

People say time heals. I'm not so sure about that. I think you become used to the pain and you incorporate it into your everyday life. You just simply get used to it. You accept it. You will never be the person you were before the death of your child, but you can be a new person. The new you will never forget your child. You will still have the sadness and the ache of wanting your child back. The new you can have a good life and find happiness and joy. You just have to allow yourself to become that person.

MARK

A Friend's Perspective

By Diane (Hauter) Savory

My dear friend, Regina, asked me to write a short story about what it was like to be a support person for her and her family when Mark, her son, passed away in a tragic automobile accident. I don't perceive myself as being a support person at all. After thirty years of friendship, we became very much like family. When Mark passed, I simply shared the grief.

This is my story as I remember it. It has to begin with Mark.

Mark was an extremely loving and caring person. He was always there to help anyone at the drop of a hat. He was the type of person that never knew a stranger. Don't get me wrong, even though Mark was loving, he was always looking for adventure and a good time. He had great humor and was more often than not, either laughing or teasing.

Mark lived life with a remarkable enthusiasm. When he entered a room, no matter who else was there, he took the spotlight. He never did it on purpose, that was just Mark. The energy that surrounded him was extremely vast.

I loved and laughed with Mark from the time he was a little boy, until he was twenty years, one month old—until the day he died. I still love Mark. I still miss the kiss on my cheek from him whenever we saw each other. I miss Mark. I will always miss him.

To say life can change in an instant is a major understatement. People go through life hearing about a young person passing and are always saddened. Still, they are also grateful that it didn't graze their own inner circle. We all do this. It's okay because, to coin a phrase, "We're only human." This is exactly what I did on the day of Mark's accident. It was a rainy summer afternoon. My habit was to watch General Hospital while getting ready for work. It was interrupted with a special report about a fatal accident on Talmadge Road. I worried and did a mental check on the whereabouts of each one of the people I hold dear. I believed everyone was accounted for and returned to my show.

It was after I was at work that the phone call came. I was told Ginny was on the phone. Ginny is a friend and is also a close friend to Regina. I was happy to hear from her, but couldn't understand why she would call me at work. She gave me the news straight and fast. Mark had been killed in a car accident, and I needed to go to Regina's house immediately. The only thing I remember about getting there was the windshield wipers swiping as fast as they could.

I was in a daze when I walked into Regina's home. The house that we had laughed and played in for so many years felt heavy and different. There were people everywhere. I couldn't understand how they all got there so fast. I turned to the kitchen before going to Regina. I needed to try to compose myself first. I felt as though I was speaking to and looking at people in some sort of a vacuum. Nothing felt real.

When I looked into the family room at Regina, I snapped into a different mode. She sat on the couch looking pale, stunned, and grief-stricken. There were absolutely no words to offer. I felt the need to sit with her and to stay as close as possible.

I love these people. They are my extended family. It was all too much to comprehend. Things were not right at all. The world had changed and would never be the same again. While sitting on the couch with Regina, my mind went to Mounir, Regina's husband. He was in Lebanon visiting family. The thought of him being told about Mark was unbearable. Mounir's love for all of his children is immeasurable. He has always been there to nurture and guide. There is absolutely nothing he wouldn't do for any of them, but he had a special feeling for Mark.

One day when we were in the kitchen, Mounir told me he always had a strong need to protect Mark and that he always worried about him. I guess a parent's instincts are usually right. I could feel chills going through my entire body. My mind kept telling me to "stay quiet, stay strong, and stay close."

Mark's brother, Rick, and sisters, Dina and Danya, were all there and had been told. Each one of them so special and so loved, each one trying to understand and make sense of what had happened. Thankfully, they were surrounded with their own friends and cousins.

Every room I went to was filled with groups of people. They were all full of grief and searching for a way to help. My place was with Regina. I would have it no other way. To leave her was unthinkable. The only words I could find for her were, "I love you." I think they sunk in because I remember her reaching for my hand and nodding.

When I would get up, it was to be with her other children. We would hold each other for a while and they would return to their friends. They knew I would spend the night. It was simply understood.

At one point, I feared that it was all too much for Regina to endure and asked if she would like to go upstairs. Her reply was, "Not yet." People would come to her and she would answer with brief, quiet words. They were usually, "Thank you." By 10:30 that night, I asked her again if she was ready to go upstairs. This time, she said, "Yes." Regina, her mother, and a few of her closest friends and family all went up together. When we came back down, Regina was in bed. Her mother stayed the night with her. Everyone had gone home. The house settled into a quiet state.

Two of Regina's lifelong friends and I spent the night in the family room. We never really slept. The shock had been too much. At times during the night, I would wander the house and check on the children. Rick chose to go to his room to grieve privately. Danya slept in Mark's bed. A couple of her close friends stayed with her. Dina had taken her baby girl, Kayla, home to her own bed.

In the family room, we would try to sleep. It was impossible. We would talk a little during the night about how to help. We would ask each other what we could do. None of us had an answer because there were no answers. We worried about Regina upstairs and we worried about Mounir. He was flying home. We knew they needed to be together. They needed each other as quickly as possible. If my own grief was unbearable, I couldn't imagine how much deeper theirs was.

The only way to help was to stay close and be there for the children. Their world had also taken a devastating change. We were part of each other's lives. I would not force myself on them, but I would be there when they wanted me. Sometimes we would hold each other. Other times we would just quietly look to each other across the room.

This was the first two days.

Mounir arrived home. The house took on another feeling. I went home. Now they had each other. The days that followed were filled with people coming and going. My visits were daily and I would go home at night.

It was when Mounir went back to work that I went into a different mode. I wanted to be with Regina. I would arrive in the morning. People were still coming to be with her. We would sit and visit with them. Other times we would talk or cry. Regina was strong for her children and continued to mother them. I was just a buffer. If I saw something or someone upsetting her, I would create a distraction.

One morning, Regina called me and said to stay home. She had some things she wanted to do. I saw that as a good sign from her, and it was. She was trying to start living again. I said a prayer for her and began re-organizing my own home.

I don't know if I did everything right or not. I do know that in times like these, you need to go with your heart. Sometimes just staying close and listening is the best thing you can do. I think it is all right to cry in front of them. We all did. We all loved Mark.

Since we spent so many years together in the kitchen, it was second nature to load the dishwasher or help prepare a meal. That was a sense of routine that we needed. If something needs to be done, just do it. Don't wait to be asked, because the person you want to help probably won't say what they need. Their thoughts are not really on routine.

When Regina and I were talking about writing this story, she said that the things that meant the most to her was when someone would see that they needed something and they would just do it. She gave the example of noticing when they were out of milk, someone just brought some. I don't remember if I did that or not, but I hope I did.

After awhile, things began settling into a routine. One of Regina and Mounir's greatest blessings was their granddaughter, Kayla. She brought sunshine and life back to all of us. One afternoon we were in the family room half watching General Hospital while playing with Kayla. We glanced across the room and noticed her little tennis shoes. They were the kind that twinkled light while she was walking in them. What caught our eye was that they were twinkling light while she was just lying on the floor by a chair. Regina and I both recognized the sign. As usual, Mark had come in during General Hospital.

I believe that although Mark is busy with life on another plane, he still finds a way to stay close in spirit. He has that much energy. There are times that each one of us can still feel his presence. With it comes a rush of amazement and a sense of well-being. I simply say, "Hi Mark, I love you!

ONLY THE GOOD DIE YOUNG

By Christine Perrine

On January 19, 1990, a wonderful little boy came into the world—Timothy Robert Perrine. He joined his one-year-old sister, Natalie, and would have another sister the following year named Stephanie. His dad, Bob, and I were thrilled. Timmy was such a happy boy. He never fussed, he loved everything we fed him, and he always had a huge smile for everyone to see. Timmy was like any little boy growing up. He loved to play with Legos, building all kinds of things wherever his imagination would take him.

Timmy was a great athlete. Whether it was football, baseball, or soccer, very little effort had to be put into it. He had natural talent and would always do well. School was not important to him. He felt he didn't have time for it. It was very unnecessary. He gave just enough effort to be an average student, but he could have excelled. What Tim did excel in was common sense.

Tim was a charmer and would always compliment people. He told me, "There is good in everyone. You just have to look for it." He was always very considerate and looked out for others. He would say, "Mom, it is good to hug someone when you meet them because a hug means so much more than a handshake." He gave the best hugs! Always a gentleman, he would give girls his jacket when needed. Kids always called him for advice. He felt he could fix any problem. Tim would be on the phone for hours into the night giving guidance when asked, and he was always there to lend an ear.

As if overnight, Tim grew from a skinny kid to a six-foot, two-inch tall, 192-pound teenager. He started to lift weights and he would come up to me and say, "Feel my chest, isn't it getting strong?" He would work so hard on making sure his body was just right, especially working on building up his neck muscles. Since he played sports, he used to tell me how the body needed certain nutrition to grow and I needed to buy certain foods so his body could work at its best performance. By high school, Tim was concentrating on only one sport—football.

In the fall of 2005, while I was driving Tim to school, he said, "Mom, I am not afraid to die." I looked at him in shock, wondering where that comment came from and why he said it. I told him I would be so sad if he died. Without hesitation, he said, "Mom, I will always love you no matter where I am." I didn't think anymore about his comment until two weeks later.

On September 14, 2005, Tim came home from football practice and felt very sick. He thought he was coming down with a cold or the flu. He did not know he was severely dehydrated from football practice, so he decided to take an over-the-counter cold and flu remedy. Before he went to bed, he felt worse. Without our knowledge, he also took a muscle relaxant he had found in our medicine cabinet. Tim died in his sleep on September 15, 2005. He was only 15 years old.

I can remember Bob took care of all the funeral arrangements. I could not even think about it. I remember my friend, Julie, paid all of Tim's funeral expenses. She is a wonderful, giving person. I can remember many friends and family came to show their support. I remember Tim's theology teacher, who was a nun, came up to me and said, "I knew this was going to happen. He was just that special type of boy." I can remember many of the boys from Tim's high school, St. Francis, came to the house. They were all so close. I remember Christ the King had so many in church that people were fainting. I remember buses of kids pulling up at the cemetery, and the funeral home saying it was one of the largest funerals they had ever had. I can remember just going through the motions, having no idea what I was doing. I can remember being in a fog. As I look back, though, I really didn't remember much.

I didn't remember the people who came to the funeral. The only way I knew they were there was because they signed the book. In the weeks and months following Tim's death, I only knew my Timmy was gone. To this day, I know Tim knew he was going to have to leave this world at an early age.

I had to go back to work one week after Tim's funeral. My boss told me to return as soon as possible. She felt the more time I took off, the worse it would be for me. I was afraid of losing my job. At work, I cried all the time. Co-workers would come by my cubicle and I would just break down. All they had to do was look at me. I was not ready to return to work. It was just too soon. I had to try to act like nothing had happened. As time went on, people at work started avoiding me. They eventually stopped coming around all together. They didn't know what to say to me.

Two months later at a meeting for my work review, my superior commented on how sad I still was. She said, "You have to get over this thing!" She didn't even address Tim as a person. He was only a "thing". I just sat there and took it. I couldn't even move. How I wish now I would have told her off and expressed my real feelings.

One day at work while shutting down my computer, I discovered the background of my screen was a picture of a gigantic rose with the date of Tim's death, September 15, 2005, printed on it. I was shocked and hysterical! I felt this was a message from Tim. When my superior saw it, she said she would "Take care of it and get it out of there." I didn't want her to do that! I pleaded with her. I felt very strongly this was my last gift from Tim. Regardless, my boss called the computer technical guy to remove it. When he came, I told him about Tim. I begged him not to remove the rose picture. He whispered to me, "I have children of my own. I will save it for you." He did. I secretly reloaded the image onto my computer without my boss' knowledge. It remains there today. I will be forever grateful to that computer tech for his kindness and compassion.

Each night for months after everyone else went to bed, I would go into our family room to cry. I would cry until at least 2:00 in the morning, or sometimes all through the night until it was time to get ready for work. I continued to do this until the early morning hours of July 4, 2006, when I realized I couldn't move my body. I could only move my eyes, and all I could see were spots. I told Bob to get me to the hospital. After a CAT scan, the doctors told me I had water on the brain which had caused a stroke. This had been brought on from excessive crying. After three days, my mobility came back. I realized I had to stop crying or I would have more problems.

Four months later, I experienced shortness of breath and I couldn't walk. Again, I went to the doctor and had a stress test. One minute into the test, I had to stop because my heart was pounding too fast. I then had a heart catheterization. It showed I had an arrhythmic heartbeat due to my grief. The doctor wanted to put me on medication, but before I made it back to my next appointment a bigger problem occurred.

During this time, I had missed my annual mammogram appointment. I had to reschedule a few weeks later. The day after my mammogram, the nurse called me crying uncontrollably. She said, "I'm sorry, Chris, the mammogram shows a lump in your right breast. You have to come back in. You don't need this. You've been through enough." I had an ultrasound and biopsy. It was cancer. I had a double mastectomy, then four months of chemotherapy. For the following year, I went through a series of surgeries for breast reconstruction. I also had a separate surgery to remove my ovaries because cancer was prevalent in my family.

The entire time, during chemotherapy, surgeries and doctor visits, I continued to work on and off. I had to, in order to keep my health insurance. It seemed like it was never going to end. This was a horrible time for me and my family. Eventually, the treatments ended, I healed physically, and I was able to be a stronger person from it.

While I was recovering from all my health issues, a friend of mine introduced me to Regina Elkhatib. She was a facilitator for a group called F.O.C.U.S. I went to a few meetings. I realized I wasn't alone in my grief. By listening to other parents who had lost a child, I found people who understood and knew my feelings. I started to heal emotionally. I realized so many people have similar tragedies. Even though each one deals with it differently, we all come to a common ground to find peace within ourselves and with one another.

I also began to notice changes in my family. Bob became more sensitive, more open, and would cry. At times we would talk, and other times we would find ourselves in each other's arms with our grief. No words were needed. To this day, certain songs will bring tears to both our eyes. I feel Bob and I have grown more in the last four years than in the 25 years we've been together.

Stephanie was only in the ninth grade when Timmy died. She is very closed about her feelings. It is difficult for her to discuss him. Natalie is more sensitive. She was only 16 years old when she lost her brother. She moved into Tim's room to be close to him. She surrounds herself with pictures, writes in her journal, talks to him, and asks him for help. She is still very connected to him. She and Tim were very close. Tim's friends were her friends. She deeply misses him.

When Tim died, he left an empty hole in my heart. With time, I realized that losing Tim made my heart grow. I know Tim is not "dead". I just feel he has gone away for a short time until we are together again. I have always been a caring individual. I felt I would go the extra mile for people. Now I'm much more sensitive, and I'm more empathetic. Now I really listen. I call people to check up on them. I make the time for people. I am not an empty shell. I don't sweat the small stuff. I also realize I don't judge people like I used to. I now know everyone has their own reasons for what they do. I feel I am a better mother and more sensitive to my girls. I look forward to the gifts my girls will give me as they grow older.

As I meet new people, I feel they have come into my life for a reason. I feel honored to have them in my life. They make me grow and see things that I might have missed without their insight. I really cherish everyone I meet. I feel I never know who might tell me something I need to hear.

There is never a moment in each day that goes by I do not think of Tim. I wish he were here with me still today, but I feel he had to leave to work on more important things. I often think of the wonderful common sense he had and how he was so beyond his years. Tim was a boy you would love to be friends with. He was so kind and considerate to all he met.

Tim has left his family and friends behind. We have honored and remembered him in so many ways. We have set up a scholarship program at St. Francis so boys who have a financial need are able to receive assistance. We only ask that the new student play football. That way, Tim's memory carries on in his school. It is nice that he continues to live through them.

As the song goes, "Only The Good Die Young." I look forward to the day I will be with Tim again. He has made me realize that there is a life after death. I feel his presence around me, and I can ask for his help and God's whenever I need it. I know they are there for me. One day we will be reunited, and I am ready for the day he calls my name.

LANDAN

By Kim Finnegan

I remember that day in early December, 2002, when my 17 year-old daughter, Lacey, called me from school where she had just arrived to break the news she was pregnant. I was upset, but there was little I could do. I was going to be a grandma at age forty-two.

Lacey graduated the following May, six months pregnant, and started that summer at the community college. The next few months went by fast and on August 15, 2003, she went into labor. We made two trips to the hospital that weekend before they finally admitted her. After two days, Landan Michael Everett Harris was born on August 17, 2003. He weighed nine pounds even. He was beautiful.

Landan came home to our house a couple days later with Lacey. He was the best baby. He smiled all the time. When he was fifteen months old, Lacey began dating Andy whom she would eventually marry. Andy and Landan bonded immediately. They were buddies from the beginning. Landan couldn't say "Andy", so he called him "E".

Landan was such a huge part of our lives. We saw him every day. On weekends, I would get him out of bed in the morning and let Lacey sleep. That was our time. I would hear him playing in his crib on those mornings and it would make me smile. I'd sneak up to the door and try to quietly open it, but he would hear the door creak and up he'd bounce. "Nana" he'd say when he saw it was me. It melted my heart. Every year I would make his birthday cake. I loved doing it for him.

Lacey and Andy set their wedding date for October 21, 2006. As the day approached, they decided to move in together. Lacey and Landan moved into an apartment with Andy on July 31, 2006. It was sad for us, but a new beginning for them. Landan had his own room complete with Sponge Bob bedding, his favorite character.

He would spend the night with Nana and Papa on weekends. A few times the phone would ring and it would be Landan. He was playing with Lacey's phone and he would hit redial and call the last person Lacey had talked to, which was usually me. I'd answer the phone and a little voice would say "Hi Nana!"

Lacey's wedding day finally arrived. Landan was the ring bearer but he was bashful, so Lacey's dad carried Landan as he escorted Lacey down the aisle. The wedding was wonderful and Landan spent the weekend with us so Lacey and Andy could have time to themselves.

In early November, 2006, we received the Toys-R-Us Beg Book. Landan was at our house that week and he saw the big toy book. On the front page were two big stuffed dolls of Dora and Diego. He came to me and pointed to them and said, "Nana, I want dat." I said, "You want that?" He said, "Uh huh." It was so precious. He also told his mom that he wanted the train set with the table. He had seen it on a commercial. Landan was with his father the weekend of November 11, so Lacey and I went to Toys-R-Us. Lacey bought him the train he wanted and I bought him the Dora and Diego dolls. He was going to be so excited when he got them for Christmas.

On November 13, Landan, Lacey and Andy came over to our house. Landan played with his aunts, ate popcorn and had fun. He seemed fine. The next day he awoke with a fever. Lacey gave him medicine and he slept on and off all day. He kept pulling at his throat and Lacey asked if his throat hurt. He said, "Uh huh." I talked to Lacey that night. I wanted to go over and check on him, but I knew Lacey had it handled. I know now that I wouldn't have known what was going on in his little body. Oh how I wish I had known.

I worried about Landan that night and as I woke the next morning, I was going through McDonald's for coffee as I dialed Lacey's phone. She didn't answer, so I began to leave a message. Lacey beeped in, so I clicked over to answer her call. It was a call that would change all our lives. Lacey was out of breath because she had run to get her phone. When she awoke, she found Landan lying on the floor beside her bed. She said he looked like he was covered with bruises. I asked if he was breathing, and she replied, "Yes." I asked, "What do you mean he looks like he is covered in bruises?" She was terrified. I said, "Call the squad, I'm on my way." I knew this wasn't good, whatever it was. I pulled out of line at McDonald's and raced to Lacey's, crying and praying.

I called Landan's father and told him to meet us at the hospital. I arrived at Lacey's apartment at the same time as the EMS. I ran into the apartment and right to Landan. He was still lying on the floor. Lacey was afraid to pick him up because every time she tried he would say, "Ouch," like he was in pain. The EMS knew something was very wrong, so they scooped him up and headed to Toledo Children's Hospital.

Landan's father and I arrived at the same time and we were put in a waiting room. Lacey was with Landan. When the nurses came to get us, it was so we could follow Landan to the PICU. They told Lacey that Landan was a very sick little boy. As they were wheeling Landan out of the ER to take him to the PICU, he looked at his mom and said, "Hold me, Mama." Lacey wanted to hold him, but she couldn't.

When we arrived at the PICU, they had us go down to the waiting room while they sedated Landan and started IV's. It seemed like it took forever. As we were waiting, an older lady came in. She introduced herself as the hospital chaplain. My heart sank. That wasn't a good sign. I knew the news would be bad. Then the doctor finally came down to talk to us. He confirmed our worst fears. He told us Landan had Bacterial Meningococcal Meningitis. He said Landan only had a ten percent chance of survival. What a shock! He was eating popcorn in my house two days ago!

Immediately, we called all the family. Some began to arrive at the hospital. Some of our close friends came to comfort us. Of course, we were all in shock. We tried to be hopeful. We were finally allowed to see Landan. His little body had tubes all over. He was sedated, but trying to fight sleep. The nurse told us to tell him to go to sleep. I said, "You can go sleepy." He shook his head and said, "Uh ah." We had to be in gowns and masks. We took turns going in his room. He looked swollen and had purple spots all over his body. He had gone into DIC.

The doctor talked to Lacey and Landan's father about treating him in the hyperbaric chamber. He explained that it would force oxygen into his body. The first time Landan went, he tried to sit up in the chamber. He fought so hard. He would go for two additional treatments. As night time arrived, family and friends started for home. Lacey, Andy, Landan's father and I stayed the night at the hospital. We barely got any sleep. Very early the next morning, family began to arrive back at the hospital. I was so tired. Lacey stepped out of the PICU to make a phone call and I went to get coffee in the waiting room. It was at this time, Landan chose to go. My husband, Mark, and Lacey's dad and stepmom, Jan, were there. Lacey's dad ran to get her, and Jan met me in the hall as I was heading back to the PICU.

"Hurry, Kim," Jan said, "Landan's heart stopped." I ran back to Landan's room. Lacey and Landan's father were standing there with my husband and Lacey's dad. The room he was in had glass sliding doors on the front. The doctor was doing chest compressions. I screamed Landan's name. I told him we were there. I turned to my husband and told him I didn't think I could do this. Lacey stood there in shock with her hand on her mouth. The doctor came out and took Lacey, Landan's father and me into the next room. He said, "We're not going to be able to save him." I said, "Is he gone?" The doctor replied, "Yes." Lacey couldn't cry. She was in shock. Landan's father began to cry. I tried to hug them both.

My heart was ripped from my chest. I began to call family and friends to tell them we had lost our beautiful Landan. We were allowed to hold him once the IV's were removed. I was the first. I kissed him. I told him how much I loved him, and that I didn't want to let him go. Family and friends began to arrive. They all took turns holding Landan. There were oceans of tears.

Lacey held him. She looked up at me from the rocking chair and said, "Mom, I don't want to go home without him." All I could say was, "I know." I knew how painful it was for me as his Nana. It had to be horrific as his mother. Landan was gone at the age of three. Lacey was only twenty-one.

We held Landan for five hours, then the nurse said it was time. Landan was swaddled in four hospital blankets with pink and blue baby feet printed on them. I asked the nurse if I could have the blankets and she said, "Absolutely." I took three of them. I gave one to Lacey, one to Landan's father, and I kept the third. Lacey asked the nurse if anyone would be with Landan until the funeral home came for him. The nurse promised she would stay with him and not leave Landan alone. A social worker at the hospital asked us what funeral home we wanted to use. We told her the one closest to our home. She called them and set up a time for us to meet the next day. We then left. What a lonely drive home.

We arrived the following day at the funeral home. To our surprise, they donated all their professional services to Landan. While we were there, the deacon of our parish, St. Rose, called and donated a plot to bury Landan. What a blessing these people were to two young parents who had just lost the joy of their lives.

So many things went through my mind. Why? What did I do? Was I not a good enough Catholic? I knew that God wouldn't take a child away from a family who loved him just because He wanted to send a message to me. My heart was trying to justify this loss.

The funeral was beautiful. The train set and the Dora and Diego doll he wanted so badly were on display. Landan never got to see them. There were a lot of cars in the funeral procession. The city police blocked traffic so we could all get to the cemetery. As we arrived at St. Rose Cemetery, there was a city police officer there to stop oncoming traffic so all the cars could enter. As Landan's hearse went by, the officer saluted. Landan would have loved that. It brought me to tears. It was a touching gesture and it meant a lot to Landan's family. We picked out a beautiful headstone with Sponge Bob on it.

Our lives have not been the same. We have managed to go on without Landan, but we had no choice. I miss him. Lacey and Andy now have another little boy. He makes my heart smile again. Landan would have been a great big brother. We will make sure he knows all about his big brother Landan.

Since Landan's passing, Lacey has delved into the online community. It first started with constructing an online memorial for Landan through a website called Memory-Of. Most of her networking with other "angel moms" came on MySpace. Lacey had already had her own personal MySpace for many years and never knew of any other parents on it who had lost their child. Once Landan passed away, she quickly realized she wasn't alone. She met a lot of other parents who had lost a child as well. I know it was very good for her to meet others who could relate to the pain she was in.

Lacey also put a lot of time, effort and grief into learning how to use a graphic program called "Photoshop". She has done beautiful graphics for herself and other "angel parents" as keepsakes of their "angel children". Lacey has even had one of her creations permanently engraved on the headstone of a little boy whose mother she met online. Lacey has also created a website to remember Landan and promote awareness of Meningitis. It is www.angellandan.com. She has made many memorial videos of Landan that are set to music.

Lacey is very active with Meningitis Angels and The National Meningitis Association, doing whatever she can to encourage vaccinating younger children against this deadly disease. She still deals everyday with the anxiety she has developed since losing Landan. She was eighteen years old when she delivered him, and was twenty-one when she buried him. She has owned her own cemetery plot since she was twenty-one. That is truly sad. I am very proud of Lacey's efforts to keep Landan's memory alive and to help others who have experienced the loss of a child.

Remembering Landan
8/17/03—11/16/06

http://www.landan-harris.memory-of.com
http://www.myspace.com/inmemoryoflandan
http://www.myspace.com/mamaxolacey
http://missinglandan0306.blogspot.com

A "HOPE" LIST
FOR THE BEREAVED

1. I wish my loved one had not passed. I **hope** to one day be able to accept their passing and to understand they continue to live on.

2. Please speak my loved one's name. I **hope** you will understand that hearing their name affirms they left their imprint on this earth.

3. I cry because of my grief, not because of something you said. I **hope** you understand tears are cleansing and are a way of expressing my love and loss.

4. If I surround myself with photos and personal items, it is because these are important to me. They are tangible connections to my loved one. I **hope** you allow me to express my loss. Please bear with me.

5. I am thankful for those who are around me when I need them the most. I **hope** you also understand if sometimes I need my own space and time alone to heal.

6. I need to talk about my loved one. They lived and were very important. I **hope** someday we can speak freely of our memories of them without sadness. I don't want my loved one to be forgotten.

7. I know you have thought about me often and my loved one's passing has also affected you. My **hope** is that we continue to share our loss.

8. There is no set timetable for grieving. I **hope** you allow me to mourn and heal at my own pace.

9. I am working very hard at my recovery. I **hope** to reach a level of understanding that will allow me to learn and grow from this experience.

10. I want you to try to understand how my life has changed. I **hope** a time will come when I will be able to find peace within myself.

11. Grief is the most difficult experience in life; therefore, I still struggle daily. I **hope** to someday be able to reinvest in life in a positive manner.

12. Depression, anger, hopelessness and overwhelming sadness are normal for me right now. Please excuse me when I'm quiet and withdrawn. I **hope** you will help me on this journey as I begin my new life without my loved one.

13. "Taking one day at a time" is good advice. Please know that right now I can only take one moment at a time. I **hope** someday to be able to look forward to the weeks and months ahead.

14. Please excuse me if I am uncomfortable in social gatherings. It is not my intention to be rude. It is very difficult for me to belong right now. My **hope** is that time, healing, and growth will help you enjoy my company once again.

15. Birthdays, anniversaries and holidays will never be the same. Even days leading up to them can be unbearable. I **hope** a day will come when I realize I hold my loved one close, not just those days, but every day of the year.

16. Please don't pressure me into doing things I am not physically and emotionally able to do yet. I am not ready. I **hope** one day I will be able to look forward to activities I once enjoyed.

17. My grief is not something that I will "recover" from. I will forever miss my loved one. I will never be the person I was before my loss. My **hope** is that I will honor my loved one by continuing to live my life in a positive manner.

18. I wish very much you could understand my loss and my grief, my silence and my tears, my void and my pain. But, I **hope** and pray daily that you will never understand.

THINGS NOT TO SAY...

These are a few statements that are often said to the bereaved with the best of intentions. Unfortunately, these comments, for the most part, are hurtful and can even anger those who have just suffered a loss. Your presence, actions and availability speak more than words.

"It was God's will."

"God needed another angel in heaven."

"They are in a better place now."

"Your loss is Heaven's gain."

"At least you have other children . . ." or *"You can have other children."*

"Let me tell you about (my bad situation) . . ."

"You must be stronger than me. If I had your loss, I would just die."

"Don't cry" or *"Don't be angry"* or any other *"Don't . . ."*

"I know exactly how you feel."

"Life is for the living."

"You need to get on with your life."

"You must be strong (for your mom, dad, kids, etc.)"

"Keep yourself busy."

"It doesn't get any better . . ." (Coming from another bereaved person)

"Time will heal."

EXPECTATIONS
FOR YOUR GRIEF...

Grief brings an intense amount of emotion that will surprise you and those around you. Your grief will not only be more intense than you expected, but it will also be evident in more areas and ways than you ever expected. Most of us are unprepared for the overall responses we have to a major loss. Our expectations tend to be too unrealistic. More often than not, we receive little assistance from friends and society.

Keep in mind the following for yourself during the healing process:

- Your grief takes more energy than you can ever imagine—you will tire.
- You will have trouble thinking and making decisions.
- Your grief involves many changes and is continually developing.
- You will feel some level of anger and guilt.
- Your grief shows itself in all aspects of life—psychological, social, physical, and spiritual.
- You may have feelings of irritability, frustration, annoyance and/or intolerance.
- You may experience grief spasms, acute upsurges of grief that occur suddenly with no warning.
- You will grieve for what you have lost already and for what you have lost for the future.

August 28, 2011

Dear Cirdy and Michael

We realize your grief is beyond words and perhaps this gift may not be timely on this very day. We would like you to keep it, though, in our hope that when you are ready you will be inspired to hear and heed the words written by others that have experienced tragic loss. Angie (Christensen) said you can call her anytime and has written her phone number on her pamphlet inside the book.

Please accept this gift in the spirit in which it is given.....the spirit of love and compassion and caring.........Jackie's Spirit.......our Lord's Spirit.

With much love and true caring from your cousin and her husband,

Susie & Johnny Rodriguez

- You may begin a search for meaning and may question your religion and/or philosophy of life.
- You may find yourself acting socially in ways that are different from before.
- Your grief will entail mourning not only for the actual person you lost, but also for all the hopes, dreams and unfulfilled expectations you hold for that person.
- Grief involves a wide variety of feelings and reactions, not just those that are generally associated with grief such as depression and sadness.
- You will have some identity confusion as a result of your loss and the fact that you are experiencing unfamiliar emotions.
- You may have a lack of self-concern.
- It is normal to feel suicidal. Fantasizing about a reunion with your loved one can help you cope. However, if you make concrete suicide plans or are concerned about your feelings, please seek help.
- Society will have unrealistic expectations about your mourning and may respond inappropriately to you.
- You may find certain dates and events bring upsurges in grief.
- Certain experiences later in life may resurrect intense grief for you temporarily.

HELPING YOURSELF WITH GRIEF...

- Make time for yourself. A regularly scheduled routine at time periods that are most difficult for you may be very helpful. Spend some time alone to bring peaceful thoughts to your mind. If you wish, pray, meditate, read, walk or exercise.

- Pace yourself. Grief takes an enormous amount of energy. Identify physical ways your body is telling you it is stressed. Try to develop healthy sleep, eating, and exercise habits. Know your limits.

- When you are ready, seek and accept support. You need acceptance and caring throughout grief. Start with family, friends, coworkers, support groups and clergy.

- Find alternative coping methods. Talking to others who have had a similar experience, writing in a journal, learning more about grief through reading, and expressing your emotions through music or art, are all types of grief work that can help.

- Honor your loved one. Establishing a memorial fund or any other remembrance service can help the grief process.

- Consider finding a way to help others. Giving of yourself may also help you feel better.

- Do not be afraid to have fun. Laughter is good medicine. Allow yourself opportunities for diversion and freshness. Children and pets are great providers of healing.

- Accept your feelings of sorrow, grief, anger, etc. Remember, this is a natural part of the healing process.

SUGGESTIONS FOR CAREGIVERS...

BE PATIENT . . .

Offering emotional and physical support to mourners is exhausting and demanding. Real support is never a "quick fix."

DON'T STAY AWAY . . .

Don't avoid mourners because their pain makes you uncomfortable, or because you are afraid of saying "the wrong thing." Silence and/or absence are interpreted as "not caring" by the bereaved.

BE AVAILABLE . . .

Try to anticipate the emotional needs of the mourner. Think about times that might be the toughest (when the child might have been coming home from school, when the spouse would have been coming home from work, Sunday afternoons, holidays, birthdays, anniversaries, etc.). Try to "be there" with a phone call, visit, dinner, etc.

BE SPECIFIC . . .

Be specific about offers to help. Don't say, "Call me if you need anything." A bereaved person cannot think clearly about their needs, and does not have the energy or desire to do physical tasks. Get groceries, clean, do laundry, pick up children, etc. Keep the engagements fairly short and give the mourner a lot of leeway in backing out at the last minute if they feel overwhelmed.

DON'T PRESSURE ...

Don't push the bereaved into doing what you think is best for them. Grief is an intensely personal experience and people must be allowed to make their own decisions on their own timetable.

DON'T GIVE ADVICE ...

Don't tell the bereaved what "works" or what your opinion is, especially on subjects of religion, society or culture.

DON'T MAKE JUDGMENTS ...

Please don't judge those in mourning or question their decisions or reactions unless you are asked for your opinion. Crying, funeral arrangements, visiting the cemetery, religious beliefs or lack of, counseling, medication, future plans, etc. are all overwhelming. Let those who are bereaved have their space to deal the best they can.

LISTEN, LISTEN, LISTEN!

The best gift you can give a bereaved person is your ability to just listen attentively to them. Even if they tell their story over and over again, it helps reinforce the reality for them. It also helps others feel their loss.

Though people die, LOVE DOES NOT!

Use common sense and heartfelt love when helping the bereaved. Ultimately, genuine love is the most powerful healing force.

CPSIA information can be obtained at www.ICGtesting.com
Printed in the USA
268511BV00001B/79/P